The nine Orders of Angels are represented
in this illuminated manuscript:

In the center, God the Father, Jesus Christ,
and the Virgin Mary.

An outer circle of the first hierarchy:
angels representing
Seraphim, Cherubim, and Thrones.

Below, the second hierarchy:
angels representing Dominations,
Virtues, and Powers.

Bottom tier, the third hierarchy:
angels representing Principalities,
Archangels, and Angels.

Source: BL YT 31, f. 40v., public domain.

Praise for *Defend Us in Battle*

Every Sunday at Mass we profess our belief in things visible and invisible. The angels and Archangels are invisible to our naked eye but to our spiritual eye we are attuned to their visible activity and working in our life. Marge Steinhage Fenelon helps us to realize the power of St. Michael as he defends us in battle against sin and how the Choirs of Angels aid us in confronting sin, especially the Seven Deadly Sins. A powerful and grace-filled novena with St. Michael and his companion angels and Archangels!

> — **Father Edward Looney**, author of *How They Love Mary: 28 Life-Changing Stories of Devotion to Our Lady.*

Marge Steinhage Fenelon's beautiful explanation and guidance on the devotion of St. Michael the Archangel is an excellent reminder of our Lord's promise in the Great Commission. In Matthew 28, Jesus tells us, "And lo I am with you always until the end of the age." The Lord is with us always of course, in the Eucharist, in Scripture, in Church teaching, in the great cloud of witnesses, and as Marge describes, all being led by this powerful Prince of the Heavenly Hosts.

> — **Teresa Tomeo,** syndicated Catholic talk show host, best-selling author, and pilgrimage leader.

Unique, thought-provoking, and utterly inspiring! *Defend Us in Battle* is a wonderful and thorough introduction to the Chaplet of St. Michael and much more. Marge Steinhage Fenelon, in her words, "offers a unique kind of prayer experience, a 'living novena' or a kind of extended guided meditation." This book also lifts the veil on the invisible realm of spiritual warfare and enlightens the reader to the power of angels — God's messengers and protectors. I highly recommend this book!

> — **Donna-Marie Cooper O'Boyle,** EWTN TV host, international speaker, award-winning journalist, and best-selling author of more than 35 books.

In this Living Novena, Marge Steinhage Fenelon emphasizes ways we can grow in virtue with the help of St. Michael the Archangel and the nine Choirs of Angels. This book is much more than a reminder to persevere in prayer; it is an invitation to live out the virtues we pray to develop.

— **Barb Szyszkiewicz**, editor at CatholicMom.com and author of *The Handy Little Guide to Prayer.*

To our detriment, the faithful have lost touch with the rich tradition of prayer through novena — nine days dedicated to prayer for a specific intention. Marge Steinhage Fenelon's unique take on this practice, through her "living novena," is engaging, powerful, and just what this world needs! Who better to take us on this journey but St. Michael — the very angel sent by God to defeat Satan? Whatever your battle, the Chaplet of St. Michael, with its invoking the Choir of Angels, will strengthen your faith and hope while growing you in holiness.

— **Allison Gingras**, *award-winning author of the Stay Connected Journals* and *Encountering Signs of Faith*, podcaster, and Catholic new media specialist.

An absolutely wonderful book! Allow Marge Steinhage Fenelon to introduce you to the Choirs of Angels in a way that will change your life and your perspective! She shares that "God acts through His helpers to form a spiritual shield around us to safeguard us from temptation and the nasty tricks and snares of Satan and his demons." Her book is a "living novena" that you can experience as a spiritual "armchair pilgrimage." The book not only instructs about the angels but shares how they can help us overcome vice and sin.

— **Emily Jaminet**, Catholic author, speaker, radio personality, wife, mother of seven, and executive director of the Sacred Heart Enthronement Network.

The activity of the unholy angels has undeniably increased in our age, making Marge Steinhage Fenelon's book necessary and timely. *Defend Us in Battle* will strengthen your devotion to each choir of the holy angels and allow you to entrust yourself unhesitatingly to their care and protection. A must-read for every Catholic engaged in the unseen but ever-present war — and that means all of us.

— **Claire Dwyer**, best-selling author of *This Present Paradise, a Spiritual Journey with St. Elizabeth of the Trinity.*

Marge Steinhage Fenelon masterfully incorporates Scripture, the *Catechism*, and the need for the Choir of Angels in your quiver for your daily spiritual battle. God gave you His angels, and Marge helps you reflect on virtue and vice with each verse and angel. Saint Michael's is a great devotion or novena, and this book can help protect you on the journey.

— **Kendra Von Esh**, speaker, faith coach, and author.

Modern times are fraught with chaos and spiritual attacks, but this is not new. Marge Steinhage Fenelon's book *Defend Us in Battle* reintroduces us to this devotion as a "living novena" with meditations to guide us in prayer. It is a powerful way to incorporate this devotion into your spiritual life.

— **Maria Morera Johnson**, author of *My Badass Book of Saints: Courageous Women Who Showed Me How to Live*

What a beautiful guide of prayer with the angels, weeding out imperfections and lifting our hearts to Heaven. Marge Steinhage Fenelon is a master at prayer and journeying through her writing while teaching us the lessons of faith. This powerful armchair pilgrimage melds our walk with God to the power that He has given His angels to lead us closer to Him.

— **Patti Maguire Armstrong**, journalist with the *National Catholic Register* and author of *What Would Monica Do?*

Even though some may choose to disagree with the Church's teaching on the existence of Satan, the current state of the world provides ample evidence that he's real and doing damage! In *Defend Us in Battle*, Marge Steinhage Fenelon introduces us to an ally infinitely more powerful than Satan: St. Michael the Archangel. By praying this living novena, based on the Chaplet of St. Michael, we no longer have to stand by and watch the evil one destroy all we hold dear. Thanks to this book, we have an effective weapon that can be used to defeat him. Highly recommended!

— **Gary Zimak**, best-selling author, speaker, and radio host.

Boy, do we need this now! In this time of anxiety, conflict, and confusion, Marge Steinhage Fenelon has given us a prayerful gift that should provide solace and hope to many. With this book, a new generation of readers can encounter this ancient devotion to St. Michael and discover an abiding spirit of trust, courage, and renewed faith. It's a blessing you'll want to revisit and share with those you love.

— **Deacon Greg Kandra**, author and blogger of "The Deacon's Bench."

Defend Us in Battle

*The Promises of St. Michael
and the Heavenly Angels*

Marge Steinhage Fenelon

Available from:
Marian Helpers Center
Stockbridge, MA 01263

Prayerline: 1-800-804-3823
Orderline: 1-800-462-7426
ShopMercy.org

Websites:
Marian.org
TheDivineMercy.org
DivineMercyPlus.org

Library of Congress Control Number: 2024933477
ISBN: 978-1-59614-616-7

Imprimi Potest:
Very Rev. Chris Alar, MIC
Provincial Superior, Blessed Virgin Mary, Mother of Mercy Province
Marian Fathers of the Immaculate Conception of the B.V.M.
Feast of the Presentation of the Lord
February 2, 2024

Nihil Obstat:
Robert A. Stackpole, STD, Censor Deputatus
February 2, 2024

Note: The *Nihil Obstat* and corresponding *Imprimi Potest* are not a certifi-
cation that those granting it agree with the contents, opinions, or statements
expressed in the work. Instead, they merely confirm that the work contains
nothing contrary to faith and morals.

Layout and Cover Design: Kathy Szpak
Cover image: iStock

Scripture quotations are from *New Revised Standard Edition Bible*, copyright
©1989 National Council of the Churches of Christ in the United States of
America.

Excerpts from the English translation of the *Catechism of the Catholic
Church* for use in the United States of America Copyright © 1994, United
States Catholic Conference, Inc. — Libreria Editrice Vaticana. Used with
Permission. English translation of the *Catechism of the Catholic Church*:
Modifications from the Editio Typica copyright © 1997, United States
Conference of Catholic Bishops — Libreria Editrice Vaticana.

To Zoran, our own St. Michael

Table of Contents

Foreword

The times are tough — we need the help of St. Michael and all the holy angels more than ever. That's why I'm so pleased that my good friend Marge Steinhage Fenelon has written this excellent introduction to devotion to St. Michael, especially by praying the Chaplet of St. Michael.

She knows from the long practice of her faith how all of us Christians are attacked by the forces of hell, either through temptation or through the more showy, spectacular sorts of attacks. Marge knows very well how important devotion to the holy angels can be for Christians living in this vale of tears, this battlefield that is the present life. After all, "Our struggle is not with flesh and blood but with the principalities, with the powers, with the world rulers of this present darkness, with the evil spirits in the heavens" (Eph 6:12). That means we need allies; we can't beat the devil and the forces of hell on our own! We must turn with trust to Heaven for aid — God, His angels, and His saints.

The Chaplet of St. Michael is a less well-known, but no less powerful devotion, asking the help of the whole host of Heaven in our struggle for virtue and against vice, as well as our struggle against evil in any form. And these days, boy, is there a lot of evil for us to struggle against! But the angels have not abandoned us. Rather, they await our invitation to act with greater and greater power to help us, our families, our parishes, and all our secular and sacred communities at every level. The worse things seem to us in the Church and the world, the more regularly and fervently we all should be praying! There aren't very many more effective ways to intercede for people than to ask the holy angels for their assistance.

After all, as Marge writes, St. Michael "made three promises to all who faithfully pray the chaplet in his honor: An escort of nine angels chosen from each of the nine Choirs of Angels when approaching Holy Communion; his continual assistance and that of all the angels throughout life; and, after death, deliverance from Purgatory for themselves and all their relations."

In this time of Eucharistic revival, what a blessing to have such an escort! What an encouragement to pray this angelic Chaplet and worthily receive Holy Communion regularly, even daily! Can you imagine how awesome it must be from a spiritual perspective to see a soul going to receive our Eucharistic Lord, accompanied by an angel from each of the nine choirs? What an incredible grace!

Also, as we approach the Jubilee Year 2025 (dedicated in a special way to Hope), we need to be faithful to prayer. Without prayer, we can have no hope, especially in these times of war, disease, and disaster. Without the active help of the holy angels, we are far more vulnerable to the traps and snares of the evil one.

It's long past time for devotion to St. Michael and his angelic brethren to take their place alongside the Mass, the Liturgy of the Hours, the traditional Dominican Rosary, and consecration to the Immaculate Heart of Mary and to St. Joseph. After all, we know that the holy angels helped Our Lady and St. Joseph in special ways during their lives on earth, as I've discussed in my books and talks over the years. Remember the Annunciation? Remember the dreams of St. Joseph? These holiest of saints didn't disdain the assistance of the angels, or attempt to do God's will on earth without angelic assistance. Even our Lord Himself was ministered to by the angels throughout His life and work on earth! (See, for instance, Mt 4:11; Lk 22:43.) How could we ever have the damnable pride to think that we could do without a relationship with the angels? If the Queen of Heaven and the first among the saints needed angelic intervention, we definitely need the angels' help, too!

It's long past time for us to throw open wide the doors, welcome in the holy angels, and ask their intercession for our loved ones and every need. We've got a real battle on our hands in the world today; let's bring out the big guns!

May God bless you! May Our Lady, Queen of Angels, and St. Joseph, Terror of Demons, pray for you!

Saint Michael the Archangel and all you holy angels, pray for us! Defend us in battle!

Very Rev. Donald H. Calloway, MIC
Vicar Provincial, Blessed Virgin Mary, Mother of Mercy Province,
Congregation of Marian Fathers of the Immaculate Conception of the B.V.M.

Introduction

I have a friend who refuses to talk about anything having to do with Satan, even in the most abstract way. When his name comes up, she either changes the subject or bows out of the conversation. Clearly, it makes her uncomfortable. I think many of us are like that. We'd rather not think about the devil, preferring instead to focus on more pleasant things. Granted, we should not dwell on Satan and his evil ways, because when we do that, we make him feel more powerful than he deserves. On the other hand, we should not ignore his existence, power to tempt us to disobey God's commandments, or ability to engage us in a spiritual battle. He is cunning and always looking for ways to turn us toward him and away from God. We need to strike a balance between — at the same time — keeping our faces toward the divine and being aware of the influence of the evil one in our lives.

While Hollywood has worked the ideas and images of resisting evil into horror and adventure films, the day-to-day reality of it is much simpler. As Christians, we're called to resist evil at all times and in all ways, from the biggest temptations to the smallest impulses. We are called by our Baptism to renounce evil and follow Christ. The *Catechism of the Catholic Church* tells us:

> By his reason, man recognizes the voice of God which urges him to "do what is good and avoid what is evil." Everyone is obliged to follow this law, which makes itself heard in the conscience and is fulfilled in the love of God and of neighbor. Living a moral life bears witness to the dignity of the person.[1]

Resisting temptation and sin isn't just a good idea; it's an obligation and part of our Christian mission and gives us dignity.

Thankfully, we're not left to our own devices in this regard! Our Lord has given us the Sacraments, particularly Reconciliation and Eucharist, to strengthen us against temptation. He's also given us heavenly helpers — the saints to intercede for us and the angels to protect and guide us. The saints are human beings who have gone before us and lived lives worthy of canonization and imitation. But angels are pure spirits without forms or bodies whose only purpose is to praise God and mediate between God and man. They have the power of thinking, willing, choosing, and deliberately loving.[2]

Saints communicate to us through their words and examples while angels communicate with us by suggesting things to our imagination, which we often call "inspiration."[3] In their spiritual form, we cannot see them but they can make themselves look like anything they want by manipulating our imagination or putting on the disguise — usually a human form; the images we see of angels with wings and halos are merely symbolic representations.[4]

God acts through His helpers to form a spiritual shield around us to safeguard us from temptation and the nasty tricks and snares of Satan and his demons. They help us to resist the sins that could damage our souls and threaten our salvation.

Among the saints and angels, St. Michael holds a prominent position in the fight against Satan and our protection against his wiles. His name means "Who is like God?" (*Mikha'el* in Hebrew) and is a question rather than an answer. When Lucifer, filled with pride and contempt, rebelled against God, it was St. Michael who cast him forever from the eternal gates. In that moment, Michael rose from relative obscurity within the eighth Choir of Angels (the Archangels) and levied God's judgment upon the evil one with the question, "Who is like a God?" His zealous defense of God's supreme might earn for him the title "Prince of the Heavenly Hosts."[5]

Saint Faustina had a special place in her heart for St. Michael and wrote in her diary, "I have great reverence for Saint Michael the Archangel; he had no example to follow in doing the will of God, and yet he fulfilled God's will faithfully."[6] On September 29, 1936 — the feast of St. Michael the Archangel — St. Faustina was visited by St. Michael, who assured her of his special protection against evil. He told her, "The Lord has ordered me to take special care of you. Know that you are hated by evil; but do not fear — 'Who is like God!'" Even after his departure, St. Faustina could feel the archangel's presence and assistance.[7]

In addition to the Sacraments, saints, and angels, we have an almost countless number of devotions available to us to fortify us on our spiritual journey. The most powerful is the Rosary, given to St. Dominic Guzman in 1208 by the Blessed Virgin Mary. Since then, she has appeared throughout the world urging us to pray the Rosary against sin and evil.

Another powerful yet lesser-known devotion is the Chaplet of St. Michael.

The Chaplet was given by St. Michael himself to a Portuguese Carmelite nun named Antónia d'Astónaco in 1751. He instructed her how to pray it and to teach others about it as well, and thus it became known as the Chaplet of St. Michael. He made three promises to all who faithfully pray the chaplet in his honor: an escort of nine angels chosen from each of the nine Choirs of Angels when approaching Holy Communion; his continual assistance and that of all the angels throughout life; and, after death, deliverance from Purgatory for themselves and all their relations.

The first time I prayed the Chaplet, I felt a great sense of peace and security. It was as if St. Michael had suddenly drawn very close to me and was reassuring me of his presence and protection. I began reciting the Chaplet of St. Michael as part of my morning prayer routine, and since then I have rarely missed a day; it's part of my stable of essential devotions.

In practicing this devotion to St. Michael, I've received an additional and unexpected gift. I've not only grown closer to St. Michael, but also to the nine choirs, or groups, of angels traditionally recognized by the Church. The Chaplet includes nine salutations (like decades of the Rosary), each addressed to one of the choirs, and each asking for a particular grace. For me, it has made the Chaplet of St. Michael more than a prayer for protection. It has made it an opportunity to learn about the hierarchy of angels and to grow in holiness and wisdom.

I marvel at God's goodness and mercy in leading me to the Chaplet of St. Michael, and I am grateful to have this opportunity to introduce it to you. We all should be concerned about the influences of evil because they are real. But we should never fear them because God is with us always and assists us through His grace and through His heavenly helpers.

I pray that you discover the peace and security that I have in the Chaplet of St. Michael and that you will introduce it to others as well. Together, we can stand strong against sin, temptation, and the influence of evil and grow in holiness and wisdom.

May St. Michael guide and protect you always!

— **Marge Steinhage Fenelon**

What is a "Living" Novena?

A novena is a form of Catholic devotion that involves offering special prayers or services for nine consecutive days (*novena* means "nine") for a particular intention. This practice can be traced back to apostolic times when the apostles and Mary gathered in the Upper Room for nine days after the Lord ascended into Heaven (see Acts 1–2). On the tenth day, the Holy Spirit descended upon them at Pentecost. Over time, particular novenas dedicated to particular saints or for particular seasons or intentions began to spring up in every time and place.

This book offers a unique kind of prayer experience, a "living" novena or a kind of extended guided meditation. By reading one chapter of this book each day, you will be able to experience a spiritual "armchair pilgrimage" that will lead you day-by-day to a greater understanding of, and growing devotion to, the nine Choirs of Angels.

Each day, as we examine one of the nine choirs, you learn about these heavenly creatures and God's design for them. Then, we unfold the salutation specific to the choir and what it means for us. Next, we explore a common kind of sin and travel deeper into our own hearts to discover our own weaknesses so that we might avoid such sin in the future. This is followed by questions for reflection. It can be intimidating to be frank with ourselves, and to truthfully admit what's going on inside of us. But unless we do that, we will not progress on our journey toward Heaven. Resolutions are included to bolster your spiritual growth. Finally, each day ends with a prayer to the angelic choir and an invocation for their heavenly assistance.

I hope that you find this "living" novena helpful on your path away from sin and toward holiness.

How to Pray the Chaplet of St. Michael

The Chaplet of St. Michael was given by St. Michael to Portuguese Carmelite nun and Servant of God Antónia d'Astónaco in the eighteenth century. During the vision, St. Michael instructed Sr. Antonia to make nine salutations to the nine Choirs of Angels. For those who pray the Chaplet in his honor, he promised an escort of one angel from each of the choirs when approaching Holy Communion.

For those who pray the Chaplet daily, he promised his enduring assistance and that of all the holy angels during their life, and after death deliverance from Purgatory for themselves and their relations.[8]

The prayer starts:

O God, come to my assistance. O Lord, make haste to help me. Glory be to the Father and the Son and the Holy Spirit.

Then one Our Father and three Hail Mary's are to be prayed after each of the following nine salutations:

1. By the intercession of St. Michael and the celestial Choir of Seraphim, may the Lord make us worthy to burn with the fire of perfect charity. Amen.

2. By the intercession of St. Michael and the celestial Choir of Cherubim, may the Lord grant us the grace to leave the ways of sin and run in the paths of Christian perfection. Amen.

3. By the intercession of St. Michael and the celestial Choir of Thrones, may the Lord infuse into our hearts a true and sincere spirit of humility. Amen.

4. By the intercession of St. Michael and the celestial Choir of Dominions, may the Lord give us grace to govern our senses and overcome any unruly passions. Amen.

5. By the intercession of St. Michael and the celestial Choir of Virtues, may the Lord preserve us from evil and falling into temptation. Amen.

6. By the intercession of St. Michael and the celestial Choir of Powers, may the Lord protect our souls against the snares and temptations of the devil. Amen.

7. By the intercession of St. Michael and the celestial Choir of Principalities, may God fill our souls with a true spirit of obedience. Amen.

8. By the intercession of St. Michael and the celestial Choir of Archangels, may the Lord give us perseverance in faith and in all good works in order that we may attain the glory of Heaven. Amen.

9. By the intercession of St. Michael and the celestial Choir of Angels, may the Lord grant us to be protected by them in this mortal life and conducted in the life to come to Heaven. Amen.

Next, one Our Father is to be said in honor of each of the following leading angels: St. Michael, St. Gabriel, St. Raphael, and your Guardian Angel.

Concluding prayers:

O glorious prince St. Michael, chief and commander of the heavenly hosts, guardian of souls, vanquisher of rebel spirits, servant in the house of the Divine King and our admirable conductor, thou who dost shine with excellence and superhuman virtue, deliver us from all evil, who turn to thee with confidence and enable us by your gracious protection to serve God more and more faithfully every day.

Pray for us, O glorious St. Michael, Prince of the Church of Jesus Christ, that we may be made worthy of His promises.

Almighty and Everlasting God, Who, by a prodigy of goodness and a merciful desire for the salvation of all men, has appointed the most glorious Archangel St. Michael Prince of Thy Church, make us worthy, we beseech Thee, to be delivered from all our enemies, that none of them may harass us at the hour of death, but that we may be conducted by him into the August Presence of Thy Divine Majesty. This we beg through the merits of Jesus Christ Our Lord.

Amen.[9]

DAY 1

Invoking the Choir of Seraphim
Resist Envy

Learning from God's Messengers:
The Choir of Seraphim

The word "seraph" comes from the word "serpent." The Bible mentions serpents on numerous occasions, and in most cases they are seen as evil or harmful creatures. In the Garden of Eden, Satan appears as a serpent to convince Eve to eat fruit from the Tree of Life with the knowledge of good and evil. In Genesis, the serpent is described as "more crafty than any other wild animal that the LORD God had made" (Gen 3:1). In his affliction, Job gives glory to God by proclaiming, "By his wind the heavens were made fair; his hand pierced the fleeing serpent" (Job 26:13).

There's a bit of a turn in the Book of Hebrews, where serpents bite and sicken the ungrateful Israelites ... until another serpent cures them. "So Moses made a serpent of bronze, and put it upon a pole; and whenever a serpent bit someone, that person would look at the serpent of bronze and live" (Num 21:9). God had sent poisonous serpents to the Israelites as a punishment for their ungratefulness. They'd been complaining about the "miserable food" (manna) that God had sent them to keep them alive in the desert. In both cases, the serpent is a powerful creature to be revered.

This image of the serpent shifts when we reach the Book of the prophet Isaiah. At that point we see the word "seraphim" used to describe celestial beings in the vision of Isaiah:

> In the year that King Uzziah died, I saw the Lord, high and exalted, seated on a throne; and the train of his robe filled the temple. Above him were seraphim, each with six wings: With two wings they covered their faces, with two they covered their feet, and with two they were flying. And they were calling to one another: "Holy, holy, holy is the LORD Almighty; the whole earth is full of his glory."(Is 6:1–3)

The seraph performs a rite of purification for Isaiah and, just as the bronze serpent healed the Israelites who had been smitten by the poisonous serpents, the seraph in Isaiah's vision heals him from sin:

> At the sound of that cry, the frame of the door shook, and the house was filled with smoke. Then I said, "Woe is me; I am doomed! For I am a man of unclean lips, living among a people of unclean lips, and my eyes have seen the King, the LORD of hosts!" Then one of the seraphim flew to me, holding an ember which he had taken with tongs from the altar. He touched my mouth with it. "See," he said, "now that this has touched your lips, your wickedness is removed, your sin purged" (Is 6:4–7).

The seraph is mentioned again in the Gospel of John, where Jesus compares Himself to the bronze serpent in the Book of Numbers. "Just as Moses lifted up the serpent in the wilderness, so must the Son of Man be lifted up, that whoever believes in him may have eternal life." In this case, the healing is from death itself.

Who Are the Seraphim?

Because of their high position in the hierarchy, the Seraphim most closely reflect the highest attribute of God as manifest in creation: His love. Like the fiery serpents in the Bible, the Seraphim are fiery creatures burning with love of God. Classical art usually portrays them as ablaze with six wings but no faces, forming a sea or ring of flame around the Holy Trinity. According to St. Jerome, they not only burn by themselves but they also inflame others with the love of God.

The Seraphim are powerful, magnificent creatures whose sole occupation is to attend the throne of God, making them part of God's royal court. The six wings are more than a visual reminder of their power, as each set has a specific purpose and meaning. Two of their wings cover their faces from the brilliance of God's glory, two cover their feet, two are used for flying, allowing them to do whatever they are called to do by God. Their constant chorus of "Holy, holy, holy" signals to the universe that God alone is holy and, in this way, fulfills a prophetic function that encourages all to worship the living God. Everything the Seraphim do springs forth from a burning love that demonstrates the perfect charity for which all Christians are called to strive.

In her *Diary*, St. Faustina described her encounter with a seraph. She had become so ill that her caregiver, Sr. David, forbade her to go to the chapel to receive Holy Communion the next day. In the morning, St. Faustina prepared herself spiritually to receive the Eucharist even though she knew she could not do so actually. Suddenly, a seraph appeared to her. She described him as being surrounded by a great light, "the divinity of God being reflected in him." He wore a golden robe and over it wore a transparent surplice and transparent stole. He carried a crystal chalice covered by a transparent veil:

> I saw at my bedside a Seraph, who gave me Holy Communion, saying these words: "Behold the Lord of Angels." When I received the Lord, my spirit was drowned in the love of God and in amazement. This was repeated for thirteen days, although I was never sure he would bring me Holy Communion the next day.

The seraph disappeared as soon as he had given St. Faustina Holy Communion.[10]

The First Salutation:
For Charity

In the first salutation of the Chaplet of St. Michael, we pray, "By the intercession of St. Michael and the celestial Choir of Seraphim, may the Lord make us worthy to burn with the fire of perfect charity." That sounds so wonderful, but what does "perfect charity" mean? When we hear the word, perhaps we associate it with giving money to the poor or an agency that helps the destitute or disaster victims. That's part of it, but only a small part. Charity has a greater meaning.

Among all the virtues, charity reigns supreme. We say this because the practice of all the other virtues depends on it. Charity — perfect love of God — motivates us to live virtuous lives despite the cost. Charity is what makes us human, and when I struggle to be charitable (which I often do), I like to go back to what St. Paul tells us. He wrote to the Corinthians:

> Love never fails. If there are prophecies, they will be brought to nothing; if tongues, they will cease; if knowledge, it will be brought to nothing. For we know partially, and we prophesy partially, but when the perfect comes, the partial will pass away. When I was a child, I used to talk as a child, think as a child, reason as a child; when I became a man, I put aside childish things. At present we see indistinctly, as in a mirror, but then face to face. At present I know partially; then I shall know fully, as I am fully known. So, faith, hope, love remain, these three; but the greatest of these is love" (1 Cor 13:8–13).

By love, St. Paul means charity, the kind of charity that urges us to put self aside and seek only the will and glory of God like the Seraphim do.

We refer to charity as one of the three theological virtues, the other two being faith and hope. We call it thus because of its importance to our spiritual growth and sanctification. It is loving God "above all things for his own sake and our neighbors as ourselves for the love of God," as the *Catechism* tells us.[11] Jesus made perfect charity a "new commandment" that encompasses all the others. He said, "This is my commandment, that you love one another as I have loved you." (Jn 15:12). And how did Jesus love us? He gave His life for us, suffering a horrifying and excruciating death on the Cross.

Whenever I withhold love from someone, I talk, think, and reason as a child. Not an enlightened child of God, but as a stubborn, childish person who wants only what is attractive to me and seeks justification in my lack of charity. When someone acts unkindly toward me, I am tempted to act unkindly toward them. I find it difficult to love someone who does not love me back. I even can find myself avoiding someone who simply rubs me the wrong way for no apparent reason. In all these cases, childishness takes over and blocks my ability to love perfectly as Jesus did.

That is not what Jesus wants for me. He desires that I remain in a state of grace, to engage in a loving relationship with Him and to love everyone for His sake. He wants that for you, too. It is no wonder, then, that we ask the Seraphim along with St. Michael to intercede for us before God so that we, too, may burn with the fire of perfect charity, as they do.

Examining the Influence of Envy

A lack of charity in our hearts can make us vulnerable to the grave sin of envy. We may often tease about being envious of someone, but it is no joking matter. Envy is sadness at the good fortune of another and joy at their evil. At its root is pride. Rather than rejoice in the fact that they have special gifts or privileges, we begrudge them their joy and wish it for ourselves. When taken to an extreme, envy can cause us to act out and deprive someone of possessions and honors through illicit means like gossip, defamation, trickery, deception, theft, physical harm, or even death.

I had a high-school classmate who seemingly had everything and was everything. She came from a well-known and well-respected family while mine was dysfunctional and seen as outsiders because we'd moved from the big city into a small rural town. This classmate — I'll call her Tonya — was pretty, popular, and smart. She was part of "the clique," a group of girls who seemed to be and have it all. Tonya was at the top of our class, excelled in sports, always made the cheerleading and pom-pom squads, was on the school newspaper and yearbook editorial staff, and got lead roles in all the school plays. Me? I had a small circle of friends and was sometimes mocked by other students. I was clumsy, chunky, second-rate in sports, passed up for the coveted cheerleading positions, never made the pom-pom squad, and never got the cherished lead roles in the plays. It seemed to me that Tonya was everything I was not and was rewarded for being "stuck up."

Then one day, word spread that Tonya had gotten pregnant by her boyfriend. What I felt inside when I heard the news confused me. All along, I had envied her and wished to be like her. But I was not wishing to be like her now. In the following months, I watched her come to school each day with her expanding abdomen and realized that her life had changed forever. While the child she carried in her womb would eventually become a great blessing, God had given her a difficult situation to grapple with for the time being. Through this situation the Lord was teaching me that envy is a dangerous trap, and that decisions about a person's fate are best left to Him. Envy hurts the self and not the other.

Envy not only affects us, but it also affects the whole Church. My sin of envy did great spiritual harm to me, and it weakened the Church since together we make up the Body of Christ. Saint Faustina noticed envy among the sisters in her own congregation, and it saddened her. She spoke to Jesus about it, and He told her, **"Instead of correcting themselves, their hearts swell with envy, and if they do not come to their senses, they plunge even deeper. A heart, which thus far is envious, now begins to be filled with hate."**[12] Jesus Himself had been the victim of envy. Pilate, Annas, Caiaphas, Herod, and the scribes and Pharisees were so envious of His power, authority, and popularity that they put Him to death.

While I did not put Tonya to death physically (I would never do that to anyone!), I longed for the death of her good reputation. I was like Pilate, Annas, Caiaphas, Herod, and the scribes and Pharisees by letting envy take my heart to places it never should have gone. I deeply regret that. Looking back, I can see how it damaged my relationship with our Lord and with a fellow human being. I wish that I had done things differently, reacted differently, and been more aware of the envy that was darkening my heart. I wish that I had known then about the Chaplet of St. Michael and had understood the need to call upon the Seraphim for the grace of perfect charity.

In their constant contemplation of God, the Seraphim burn with love and embody perfect charity. Their closeness to the Blessed Trinity and their complete devotion to the Triune God makes it impossible for them to experience envy. In their burning magnificence, they have the power to protect us from the temptation to envy and help us up out of the abyss if we have fallen into it.

Facing Your Personal Challenges

Living in perfect charity is a tremendous, and sometimes taxing, aspiration. The devil knows this and so will use his tricks to tempt us into becoming envious of others. Envy circumvents charity by altering our impression of the other person, causing us to judge them unfairly, just as I had unfairly judged my high-school classmate. If someone has something we do not, we begrudge them and wish it were our own. After all, why should they have something we don't? We tell ourselves that we work just as hard and deserve just as much as they do. When others frequently laud someone else for their talents and qualities, we might feel resentful that our talents and qualities receive less admiration. To take the sting out of our envy and justify our own scorn, we convince ourselves that the person somehow dishonestly or unworthily achieved their goals or obtained goods.

Envy can creep up even in our families and friendships. For instance, we can become irritated and envious of the person who always seems to win the game or get the upper hand in an argument. What we really want is for them to lose the game or give into the argument so that we can have the upper hand. It sounds simple and inconsequential, but even the tiniest bit of envy can set us up to become habitually envious of others.

Avoiding envy requires a stark examination of our judgment and an honest evaluation of our relationship with God. Judging others makes us feel better about ourselves — on the other hand, needing to feel better about ourselves indicates a lack of genuine self-worth as a beloved child of the Father. The remedy is to turn our attention to God, contemplating His divinity and allowing our hearts to begin burning with love for Him. The closer we get to God, the more our hearts will burn and the more secure in His love we will be.

Questions for Reflection

- In what kinds of situations do I most struggle with envy? What is it about them that causes me to falter?

- Is there someone in my life I frequently find myself envying? Are there particular things I envy about them? Why?

- Is there a pattern to my envy? What does this say about the way I feel about myself?

- What does my relationship with God look like? Do I burn with love for Him? What can I do to increase my love?

Resolutions

Spend at least 10 minutes meditating on the Scripture passage below. Try to put yourself in the place of Isaiah, observing the magnificent Seraphim who are burning with love of God.

> In the year that King Uzziah died, I saw the Lord, high and exalted, seated on a throne; and the train of his robe filled the temple. Above him were seraphim, each with six wings: With two wings they

covered their faces, with two they covered their feet, and with two they were flying. And they were calling to one another: "Holy, holy, holy is the LORD Almighty; the whole earth is full of his glory." At the sound of that cry, the frame of the door shook, and the house was filled with smoke. Then I said, "Woe is me; I am doomed! For I am a man of unclean lips, living among a people of unclean lips, and my eyes have seen the King, the LORD of hosts!" Then one of the seraphim flew to me, holding an ember which he had taken with tongs from the altar. He touched my mouth with it. "See," he said, "now that this has touched your lips, your wickedness is removed, your sin purged."

Make an act of charity toward someone you tend to envy or judge unfairly. For example, say a Rosary for their intentions or reach out to them with a kind gesture.

Invoking the Seraphim

O, Holy Seraphim,

Of all the Choirs of Angels, you are closest to God and most closely reflect His love. I want to burn with love as you do, but my human weakness gets in the way. I too succumb to the temptations of the devil and too easily fall into the sin of envy. Guide me away from envy and toward perfect charity so that I might constantly glorify God as you do.

By the intercession of St. Michael and the celestial Choir of Seraphim, may the Lord make me worthy to burn with the fire of perfect charity.

Amen.

DAY 2

Invoking the Choir of Cherubim
Resist Acedia

Learning from God's Messengers:
The Choir of Cherubim

Of all the biblical prophets, Ezekiel was most inclined toward visions, symbolic actions, and what some might describe as trances. His actions could seem exaggerated or theatrical, yet his purpose was to give visible form to the message he bore for the Israelites. He ate the scroll upon which the prophecy had been written to show his assimilation of the contents (see Ezek 3:1–3). He pantomimed Israel's punishment by laying on his left side for 390 days (see Ezek 4:4). He even was struck dumb for a while (see Ezek 3:26). All of this was in hope that wayward Israel might turn back to God after having apostatized, lest it be demolished, as was Judah.[13]

With Ezekiel's aptitude for spiritual revelations, it's no wonder he was the gifted recipient of visions and experiences of the Cherubim:

> Then I looked, and above the dome that was over the heads of the cherubim there appeared above them something like a sapphire, in form resembling a throne. He said to the man clothed in linen, "Go within the wheelwork underneath the cherubim; fill your hands with burning coals from among the cherubim and scatter them over the city." He went in as I looked on. Now the cherubim were standing on the south side of the house when the man went in; and a cloud filled the inner court. Then the

glory of the LORD rose up from the cherub to the threshold of the house; the house was filled with the cloud, and the court was full of the brightness of the glory of the LORD. The sound of the wings of the cherubim was heard as far as the outer court, like the voice of God Almighty when he speaks (Ezek 10:1–5).

Who Are the Cherubim?

For as much as the word "love" can be attributed to the Seraphim, the word "light" can be attributed to the Cherubim. Filled with the brightest light of Paradise, they are learned creatures who have special knowledge imparted to them by Divine Wisdom Himself. In fact, their name means "all-knowing ones." Because of their light and knowledge, they are well-suited to instruct us in the ways of sanctity, as they are especially perceptive of God's relationship with mankind.[14] The prophet Ezekiel described them as figures with eyes on all sides (see Ezek 1:18). That's a far cry from the sweet, pudgy winged babes that grace Valentine's Day cards!

The Cherubim are the first angels mentioned in the Bible and the choir most often referred to in sacred writings. After Adam and Eve's expulsion from the Garden of Eden, God sent angels to guard its gates and protect the Tree of Life. It could be that there were many types of angels sent, but the Cherubim are mentioned by name:

Then the LORD God said, "See, the man has become like one of us, knowing good and evil; and now, he might reach out his hand and take also from the tree of life, and eat, and live forever" — therefore the LORD God sent him forth from the Garden of Eden, to till the ground from which he was taken. He drove out the man; and at the east of the Garden of Eden he placed the Cherubim, and a sword flaming and turning to guard the way to the tree of life (Gen 3:22–24).

The symbolism in this scene is striking. Adam and Eve's sin was born of an inordinate desire for knowledge. They ate the fruit of the Tree of Life because they wanted to know what God knows, and to be like Him in power. Is it not fitting, then, that they should be expelled from the Garden by members of the angelic choir who had been given the gift of true knowledge?

We find the same symbolism in Exodus when God gave Moses instructions for building the Ark of the Covenant. The detailed instructions included the exact dimensions and materials to be used, and specified that it must have a mercy seat that was to be adorned with two carved Cherubim facing each other. The ark was to hold representations of God's presence among His people: a golden urn holding the manna (or bread from Heaven), Aaron's staff that budded, and the tablets of the covenant, or the Ten Commandments.[15] As with the Garden of Eden, the Ark of the Covenant was a place of encounter with the Almighty, and the mercy seat is representative of God's throne:

> Then you shall make a mercy seat of pure gold; two cubits and a half shall be its length, and a cubit and a half its width. You shall make two cherubim of gold; you shall make them of hammered work, at the two ends of the mercy seat. Make one cherub at the one end, and one cherub at the other; of one piece with the mercy seat you shall make the cherubim at its two ends. The cherubim shall spread out their wings above, overshadowing the mercy seat with their wings. They shall face one to another; the faces of the cherubim shall be turned toward the mercy seat. You shall put the mercy seat on the top of the ark; and in the ark you shall put the covenant that I shall give you (Ex 25:17–21).

King Solomon continued the Cherubim theme in building the Temple centuries later. The Temple was to be a house for the Lord, with an inner sanctuary within it that would hold the Ark of the Covenant. The entire house, including the inner sanctuary, was overlaid with gold. Solomon commissioned two 10-cubit-high (approximately 15 feet) Cherubim with 10-cubit wingspans to be carved of olivewood and overlaid with gold. The walls of the house were carved all around with Cherubim, palm trees, and open flowers. It's also interesting to note that in biblical times, palm trees were a symbol of victory.[16]

Given what we know about the Cherubim as guardians of the holy places, it could be speculated that the angels encountered by Mary Magdalene on Easter morning were Cherubim:

> But Mary stood weeping outside the tomb. As she wept, she bent over to look into the tomb; and she saw two angels in white, sitting where the body of Jesus had been lying, one at the head and the other at the feet. They said to her, "Woman, why are you weeping?" She said to them, "They have taken away my Lord, and I do not know where they have laid him" (Jn 20:11–13).

Although Mary did not initially see Him, our Lord was nearby, offering explanation for the angels' presence. Immediately after her brief exchange with them, Mary turned to find Jesus standing there.

Based on the above Scripture passages, it would be reasonable to expect the presence of Cherubim in the holy places we encounter today, such as our parish churches where Jesus waits in the tabernacle, Eucharistic Adoration and processions, and administration of the Last Rites.

The Second Salutation:
For Christian Perfection

The Cherubim's attributes of light and special knowledge of Divine Wisdom suggest the reason we ask their intercession for Christian perfection in the second salutation of the St. Michael Chaplet. Because they gaze upon perfection — God — unceasingly night and day, one would think that they are well-versed in the state of perfection, and so we turn to them for help in becoming as perfect as we possibly can so that we may live in Eternity with God.

There are two times in Scripture when Jesus explicitly directs us to strive for perfection. The first is during His Sermon on the Mount. After teaching His disciples the Beatitudes, He gave examples and instructions for becoming perfect regarding evangelization, the Law and the Prophets, anger, adultery, divorce, taking oaths, retaliation, and finally, love of our enemies. He ended His address with a directive to become perfect as the Heavenly Father is perfect:

> You have heard that it was said, "You shall love your neighbor and hate your enemy." But I say to you, love your enemies and pray for those who persecute you, so that you may be children of your Father in heaven; for he makes his sun rise on the evil and on the good, and sends rain on the righteous and on the unrighteous. For if you love those who love you, what reward do you have? Do not even the tax collectors do the same? And if you greet only your brothers and sisters, what more are you doing than others? Do not even the Gentiles do the same? Be perfect, therefore, as your heavenly Father is perfect" (Mt 5:43–48).

To love like that is indeed Christian perfection. Likewise, our calling to be the "salt of the earth" requires us to be vigilant about our thoughts, words, and actions, making certain to always exemplify pure Christian principles (even when we think we are alone, or no one notices). Our Lord's warning about the Law and the Prophets reminds us that not only does disobeying the Commandments endanger our salvation, but so does encouraging others in disobedience. At least to most people, it is obvious that murder is a grave sin. In this scene, Jesus tells us that not only is murder sinful, but so is anger and discord even if we do not act out our feelings. The act of adultery itself is sinful, but so is remarriage after divorce (unless nullity is determined)[17] and simply looking lustfully at or thinking lustfully about another human being. When Jesus warned against taking oaths, He meant that we must bind ourselves only to God, and not to humans or evil spirits, by following His will above all. Revenge or retaliation also are obstacles to Christian perfection because they prevent us from allowing God to govern our lives and perhaps the lives of others, too.

Jesus goes so far as to say that we should cut off any part of our body that causes us to sin. Does He want us to mutilate our bodies? No. He uses this as a graphic example of the absolute necessity to root out any causes of sin in our lives for the sake of Christian perfection.

The second time Jesus explicitly gives a directive for perfection is during His encounter with the rich young man. He approached our Lord, seeking the best way to achieve eternal life. Jesus told him that the primary way is by obeying the Commandments, but that there is more to it than that:

> Jesus said to him, "If you wish to be perfect, go, sell your possessions, and give the money to the poor, and you will have treasure in heaven; then come, follow me." When the young man heard this word, he went away grieving, for he had many possessions (Mt 19:21–22).

Here Jesus refers to both physical and spiritual poverty, pointing out the need for us to become empty of self, of desires for fame and glory, and of material goods and comforts. Unless we can do that, we will fail to attain Christian perfection.

Examining the Influence of Acedia

Acedia, or spiritual sloth, is the opposite of Christian perfection and one of what the Church calls the *capital sins* because it paves the way for other serious sin. The *Catechism* describes acedia as "a form of depression due to lax ascetical practice, decreasing vigilance, carelessness of heart."[18]

In his Letter to the Romans, St. Paul coined the phrase, "the spirit indeed is willing, but the flesh is weak," and that is a good description of acedia. When a person is struggling with spiritual sloth, they become so discouraged that they refuse the joy that comes from God and are even repelled by divine goodness. For them, God holds no promise of hope and there is no enthusiasm in practicing the faith. They doubt the providence and power of God, unable to believe that God cares about them or would do anything to help them. They see no value in praying or going to church because they don't think it will do any good. We are all acedic from time to time, but it becomes an occasion of serious sin when we allow it to overcome and defeat us. Because of this, acedia is a threat to our prayer life and to our striving for Christian perfection.

While I have never experienced true acedia, I have experienced something similar that helps me to understand people who suffer with it. A few years ago, I was working on a very difficult project and, at the same time, experienced a series of mishaps and calamities that affected my whole family. I had had such things happen before while working on a book, but this time was different. This time it came so fast and furiously that it barely left my husband and me time to breathe. To me, it felt as though the evil one was trying to deter me from finishing the manuscript. As I usually do, I had consecrated that project to our Blessed Mother, entrusting it to her care. When the mishaps began, I more frequently received the Sacraments and stepped up my prayer life, including prayers of binding and deliverance to protect myself and my family from any possible evil. I explained to my editor what was going on and asked for her prayers. Not only did she begin praying for us, but the entire staff joined in. Additionally, I sought help from our parish priest who was well versed in spiritual warfare. When I explained what was going on, he confirmed that what my family was experiencing was not coincidence but true spiritual warfare. Our priest and deacon joined us in praying and assisted by blessing and saying binding and deliverance prayers throughout our entire house and property. Certain aspects of the warfare calmed down a bit, but others raged on, and I began to wear out. I never stopped praying but I did begin to question whether God would rescue my family from this battle or allow it to continue. In essence, I was doubting His reasoning.

I finally got to the point that I just could not go on any longer. The next day I told my editor that I wanted to stop working on the book. I even suggested that the publisher find another writer to complete the work. She gave me a counter-offer. She suggested that I put the book aside for the time being, take some time off, rejuvenate myself and my family physically and spiritually, and then proceed when I was ready. That's exactly what I did, and in time I was not only ready but eager to return to the project. In hindsight, I'm sad and even a bit embarrassed that I allowed myself to be brought so low that I not only doubted God but nearly refused His will for me.

Facing Your Personal Challenges

Whether we experience spiritual sloth willfully because of negligence or accidentally as I almost did while working on my book, the remedy is the same. We need to reach out for God's help. That's probably the last thing anyone steeped in acedia wants to do, but it is what they need most. It is what I needed most when I struggled with it. It's crucial for us to remember that whether we feel Him near or not, God is always there beside us. While we might want to completely throw in the towel, we must push through to continue praying and to receive the Sacraments. Remember that prayer doesn't have to be long or intense. It just needs to happen at all.

Our Lord doesn't want us to fall into acedia, and He gladly will help any soul in distress; it just might not be exactly the way that soul prefers. If you are in such a state, try a short, simple, exclamatory prayer once per day. Perhaps it could be something like, "God, help me." And if even that is too much, a simple "Help me!" will do. God will know exactly what you mean by that.

Acedia is often mistaken as laziness, but it's far from that. A person suffering from acedia can seem like a productive individual. They can go about their day, tending to obligations and responsibilities and caring for loved ones. They may appear engaged in life on the outside, but inside they have disengaged from their spiritual life.

Acedia isn't about activity, it's about attitude. A better way to describe it is indifference resulting from loss of hope. We stop trusting God and caring about our relationship with Him. We can be so busy that we are distracted from joy in the

Lord and in His Love, or we can choose to engage in work or activities that disrupt or even prevent prayer and reception of the Sacraments. This kind of attitude seems to be prevalent in our culture, and so we might expect that there are many, many people who have fallen into acedia. The empty pews in parish churches, short (if any) lines at the confessionals, declining numbers of Catholic weddings and Baptisms, and the absence of God from public life all speak to rampant acedia. We can begin to change those hearts by first changing our own by seeking the help and protection of the Cherubim and invoking their intercession for the gift of Christian perfection.

Questions for Reflection

- Have I been tempted toward spiritual sloth? Have I ever been overcome by acedia?

- What were the circumstances that led to that? If there have been multiple such situations, is there a pattern?

- What led to my release from acedia? What made it better?

- Would I recognize the onset of spiritual sloth? How might I avoid it?

Resolutions

Everyone gets a little lazy with their prayer life from time to time. Most of us experience spiritual dryness here and there throughout our lives. Do some research and find a prayer that you can use during such times. The length doesn't matter. What matters is what that prayer means to you. Make a copy of it and place it where you'll easily be able to find it when you need it. This will be your go-to prayer for fighting acedia.

Invoking the Cherubim

O, Holy Cherubim,

You are the guardians of sacred places, the all-knowing beacons of light. You have been imparted superior knowledge by Divine Wisdom Himself, and thus you are uniquely able to instruct me in the ways of Christian perfection.

I ask you, please, to become the guardians of my sacred place — my soul in which our Lord Jesus dwells. Protect me from the clutches of spiritual sloth, defend me against all forms of acedia. Let me never lose hope in God or become indifferent toward His Love.

By the intercession of St. Michael and the Celestial Choir of Cherubim, may the Lord grant me the grace to leave the ways of sin and run in the paths of Christian perfection.

Amen.

"The Holy Trinity with St. Michael Conquering the Dragon" by Pietro da Cortona, 1666. Public domain.

DAY 3

Invoking the Choir of Thrones
Resist Pride

Learning from God's Messengers:
The Choir of Thrones

Saint Paul wrote to the Colossians about the supremacy of Christ, explaining to them that Jesus is primary, the "firstborn of all creation." As the Second Person of the Holy Trinity, He existed before anything else did. Therefore, all of creation was created by His power and for His purpose — even the Choirs of Angels:

> He is the image of the invisible God, the firstborn of all creation; for in him all things in heaven and on earth were created, things visible and invisible, whether thrones or dominions or rulers or powers — all things have been created through him and for him. He himself is before all things, and in him all things hold together (Col 1:15–17).

In the above passage, Paul specifically mentions the Thrones along with the Cherubim and perhaps the Principalities (rulers) and Powers.[19] His point is to demonstrate that even the highest Choirs of Angels were created by God and must submit to Him.

Who Are the Thrones?

The Thrones are the third choir in the hierarchy of angels. As their name implies, we can think of the Thrones as beings who form the seat — throne — of God's authority and mercy, just as a human sovereign would sit upon a physical throne. Saint Thomas Aquinas gives four things to consider in relation to the Thrones. First, physical thrones are raised above the earth upon stairs or a platform of some kind, for example. This places the sovereign above his or her subjects and the rest of the royal court, drawing attention to their rank of honor. The Thrones also are raised up in that they have an immediate knowledge of divine works, placing them above human beings and the other Choirs of Angels. Second, Thrones demonstrate stability, power, and strength, and attest to the authority of those who sit upon them. The Choir of Thrones symbolize God's strength but, in turn, are strengthened by Him. Third, a throne bears the person of authority, whereas the Choir of Thrones "bear" or receive God within themselves. Finally, the shape of a throne is open on one side to receive the person of authority, so the Thrones are open to receive and serve God.[20]

From their thrones, sovereigns issue their ordinances and judgments, thus governing the kingdom or empire. So, too, the Thrones form the "seat" from which God exercises His divine authority and majesty and issues His ordinances and judgments. It is through them that God accomplishes His judgments. In the early Church, God's glory typically was represented by an image of an empty throne with a radiant cross mounted above it that appeared behind the altar and above the seat of the bishop. This image stood for Christ the King, who is the Lord of all and Judge of both the living and the dead. However, His judgment seat also is a seat of mercy since Christ redeemed the world by His Cross. The throne also is a symbol of stability, and because the Thrones act as God's throne in Heaven, they, too, are a symbol of stability and always are depicted as "rolling" across the heavens rather than "flying."[21]

In his book *The Holy Angels*, Jesuit Fr. Raphael O'Connell describes the appropriateness of the Throne's name:

> It expresses, then, a certain aptitude and fitness on the part of those glorious spirits to become the dwelling of the Most High, and the seat of his majesty.

It implies a disposition on their part of wondrous purity and detachments, which prepares them to be as thrones, whereon God sits, and whence his majesty shines forth whilst he rules and passes judgment on his creatures.[22]

The Third Salutation: For Humility

Our Lord spoke many times about humility and the necessity for us to be humble. In the Beatitudes, He assured us that those who are poor in spirit (humble) will inherit the Kingdom of Heaven. "Blessed are the poor in spirit, for theirs is the kingdom of heaven," He told His disciples (Mt 5:3). He used a child as the model for the kind of humility He expects from us if we want to spend eternity with Him:

> At that time, the disciples came to Jesus and asked, "Who is the greatest in the kingdom of heaven?" He called a child, whom he put among them, and said, "Truly I tell you, unless you change and become like children, you will never enter the kingdom of heaven. Whoever becomes humble like this child is the greatest in the kingdom of heaven" (Mt 18:1–4).

In putting ourselves last in the spirit of humility, we become the greatest of Christ's followers.

However, Jesus did not leave us to our own devices in this striving. He pointed to Himself, explaining that, even though He is the King of Kings, He is "gentle and humble of heart." It is from His example that we learn true humility, and it is from Him that we gain the strength and guidance to pursue it. "Take my yoke upon you and learn from me; for I am gentle and humble in heart, and you will find rest for your souls. For my yoke is easy, and my burden is light," He assured us (Mt 11:29–30). Jesus knows our hearts, and He knows what a challenge true humility can be for us. And so He is there waiting to accompany us along the way.

The Thrones are the perfect example of humility. With their place of honor in Heaven as the closest to God — so close that they bear His countenance as if they formed a physical throne for the Almighty — they rise above the other Choirs of Angels. Yet they accept no honor for themselves. Instead, they point to God as the One who deserves honor, devoting themselves entirely to loving, worshipping, adoring, and glorifying Him. I can easily imagine, were it possible, that if we interviewed any of the Thrones, they would shun the attention and refuse any accolade. They would make it clear that they are "not such a much" in the overall scheme of things and merely performing the duties expected of them. They would — and I expect still do — demonstrate profound meekness.

For this reason, we seek the Thrones' intercession for the kind of humility they demonstrate and that our Lord embodies in the third salutation of the St. Michael Chaplet. We ask not just that we are granted humility, but that our hearts become infused with it so that we are always truly humble in all things.

Examining the Influence of Pride

The Book of Proverbs had stern words about pride: "All those who are arrogant are an abomination to the LORD; be assured, they will not go unpunished" (Prov 16:5). Later in the same chapter of Proverbs, we are warned, "Pride goes before destruction, and a haughty spirit before a fall" (Prov 16:18). By "destruction" is meant not only our material demise but also our eternal demise.

Pride is one of the cardinal sins — or sins that lead to other serious sins and vices — and Jesus warned His disciples about them:

> And he said, "It is what comes out of a person that defiles. For it is from within, from the human heart, that evil intentions come: fornication, theft, murder, adultery, avarice, wickedness, deceit, licentiousness, envy, slander, pride, folly. All these evil things come from within, and they defile a person" (Mk 7:20–23).

The scribes and Pharisees had just accused Jesus and His disciples of having ignored the Jewish laws about purification before eating. They equated such practices with a person's

worthiness before God and adherence to the Ten Commandments. In their eyes, because Jesus and His followers had not
followed the prescribed customs, they were sinners who broke
God's law. Our Lord, disturbed by their hypocrisy, admonished
them for their pridefulness. He explained that real sinfulness
comes from what lies within a person's heart and not from
making a show of adhering to customs that have no intrinsic
religious meaning. The scribes and Pharisees, He revealed, did
not follow the law because they loved God, but because they
wanted to appear more prestigious and devout than others.

Evil actions stem from the seeds of evil that lie within.
Pride is such an evil, as it festers within us and gives rise to
other sins that will threaten our salvation. Pride is so dangerous, in fact, that it can lead to envy (also a cardinal sin), war,
and even hatred of God.[23] Pride is antithetical to God's love
and refutes His goodness.

Prideful people mistakenly believe that their goodness
and excellence are generated by their own power, refusing to
admit that they come from God. Prideful people generally are
too stubborn to change their ways because they will not admit
that they have flaws, so they continue to repeat the same pat-
terns of behavior even though they may be doing things that
will cause hardship for themselves and others. They tend to
pass the blame on to others rather than take responsibility for
their words and actions. They demand respect and honor even
though they do not deserve it.

King Herod the Great is a good example of a prideful
person. He reigned over Judea during Jesus' lifetime and was
quite proud of his title and himself. When the Magi appeared
in Jerusalem asking for the Child who had been born King of
the Jews, Herod became anxious because he feared this Child
might rob him of his power and prestige. He called together
the chief priests and scribes and learned from them that this
King was to be born in Bethlehem, which was part of Herod's
realm. He secretly met with the Magi, bidding them to return
and let him know where the Child was so that he, too, could
pay them homage. The Magi, however, could see through
Herod's façade and so did not return with news of the new

King's location. They saw Herod for what he was — a bitter, prideful person — and they knew he was up to no good. They took another route home and avoided Jerusalem completely. The Magi's decision so enraged Herod that he ordered the slaughter of every male child under two years old throughout his kingdom. Herod's pride caused the deaths of innocent children, destroyed families, spread sorrow over the land, and put his own salvation at risk.

Pride takes many forms and exists in varying degrees among individuals. Some people are inherently prideful (like Herod the Great), causing destruction and long-term separation from God's love and grace. Most of us, however, are prideful on occasion, not habitually.

Pride arises when we feel we deserve something others do not; resent others who have more than we do; discredit other's qualities and achievements; or when we wish that someone who has wronged us would receive their "just rewards" by having something bad happen to them. We are prideful when we refuse to acknowledge our mistakes or admit our shortcomings and wrongdoings. Pride comes into play when we withhold forgiveness or won't back down in an argument. We mistakenly believe that doing so would somehow affect our own worth or reputation. Pride invades our hearts when we think we are somehow better than someone else, either in large or small ways. Due to our human weaknesses, pride is a part of our daily lives whether we recognize it or not.

Facing Your Personal Challenges

One of the hardest things for me to do is ask for help. To be honest, I would rather go without getting something done or having something I need than approach someone to help me out. On the rare occasions that I did ask for help, it was only because it was a serious situation, and I had no other choice. I do not ever want to admit to myself or others than I am in any way weak, needy, or incapable.

Let me give you an example. A few years ago, I had major spine surgery requiring a prolonged period of recovery. The surgery itself was a complete success, but there were complications with the incision, and it had to be opened again and allowed to re-heal, a process that took almost six months. During that time, daily cleansing and medication had to be applied and the wound redressed, which was a very involved endeavor.

Despite all of that going on, I did not want to ask for help, even though my husband was more than willing to take care of me! Pride was getting in my way, but I had no choice if I wanted to fully recover. And I certainly desired that! I longed to resume caring for my family, spending time with friends, getting back on the speaking circuit, writing more books, and continuing my apostolate. Accepting my husband's help was the only way that would happen. I cannot tell you how humbling it was for me to accept his assistance with my daily needs, from personal care to medical care to moral support.

While some may refer to it as stubbornness, pride is the real root of this character flaw of mine. It is prideful — and ridiculous — to resist help from others because of the way they might see me, or I might perceive myself. Everyone needs help from time to time, and no one is always capable and in all ways. That is not a realistic expectation of anyone, including myself.

Perhaps your prideful tendencies look different from mine. Do you hate to lose an argument? Does it upset you when someone points out that you were wrong about something? Are you put off by the less fortunate, turning away rather than extending kindness toward them? Does it irritate you when someone else gets an honor or promotion that you thought you deserved? These are all ways that pride encroaches on our lives, and there are countless others. We must always be vigilant, watching for pridefulness creeping up on us and praying for the grace to resist it.

Questions for Reflection

- How do I handle competition and arguments? Do I always have to come out on top?
- What is my reaction when I encounter people who are less fortunate or seemingly less educated than I am? Do I blame them for their own misfortune?
- Do I like to brag about my talents, skills, possessions, income, or accomplishments?
- In what ways am I like Herod the Great?

Resolutions

Read the passage about Herod the Great's pride in the Gospel of Matthew (2:1–12). Consider what most touched your heart as you read it. Then make a list of your tendencies toward pride and present it to the Lord. Ask Him for the grace to resist those tendencies and then ask Him to replace them with true humility.

Invoking the Thrones

O, Holy Thrones,

You emanate perfect humility despite your high place in Heaven. What a great honor it must be to be so close to God that you become as though you were a physical throne for Him! Your position in Heaven allows you to be strengthened by God in a direct way, making you a symbol of His strength. You demonstrate stability and power and have a knowledge of the divine that I cannot comprehend. It would seem, by human standards, that you would have a right to be prideful, but you are not.

My dear angelic friends, I often struggle with pride, and I need your help to root it out of my heart and avoid occasions of pridefulness. Please pray for me, that I may grow strong against pride. Help me to be aware of my prideful tendencies so that I may counter them before they move me to prideful thoughts and actions. I want to be as humble as you, but my human weaknesses cause me to falter.

By the intercession of St. Michael and the celestial Choir of Thrones, may the Lord infuse into my heart a true and sincere spirit of humility.

Amen.

DAY 4

Invoking the Choir of Dominions
Resist Impurity

Learning from God's Messengers:
The Choir of Dominions

The Dominions, also known as Dominations, are the first choir in the second hierarchy of angels. They are followed by the Virtues and Powers and have authority to direct them just as the Seraphim have authority over the Cherubim and Thrones. As St. Thomas Aquinas wrote in his *Summa Theologica*, "But among the angels some rule over others; and so one order is called that of 'Dominations.'"[24]

The name "dominion" reflects their mysterious nature and purpose and suggests a higher order of intelligence and the extraordinary duties with which they are charged. With their position, they are given complete freedom in their authority over the choirs below them. They are a reflection of our Lord's authority, as St. Paul wrote to the Ephesians:

> God put this power to work in Christ when he raised him from the dead and seated him at his right hand in the heavenly places, far above all rule and authority and power and dominion, and above every name that is named, not only in this age but also in the age to come (Eph 1:20–21).

By rising from the dead, Jesus displayed His dominion over all creation and for all time. Because of their closeness to him, the Dominions share in Christ's authority and power by their loyalty and service to Him.[25]

Who Are the Dominions?

In the Dominions, we see a clear example of the Church's teaching that God works through secondary causes. Despite their power and position, the Choirs of Angels number among God's secondary causes, working through Him rather than their own accord.

God is the sovereign master of His plan. But to carry it out, He also makes use of His creatures' cooperation. This use is not a sign of weakness, but rather a token of Almighty God's greatness and goodness. For God grants His creatures not only their existence but also the dignity of acting on their own, of being causes and principles for each other, and thus of cooperating in the accomplishment of His plan.[26]

As secondary causes, the Dominions' focus is the stewardship and governance of the universe and in particular the workings of divine power. They are appointed to be the coordinators of all the angels who deal with creation.[27]

On earth, leaders of kingdoms, provinces, and countries are vulnerable to tyranny and oppression. Rulers and governments seek to dominate one another for the sake of land, wealth, or control, often leading to conflict or even war. Such is not the case in the Heavenly Kingdom. The Dominions' intentions are pure (as are the intentions of all the choirs) despite their power and position as coordinators of the work of the other angels. Their purity prohibits them from becoming tyrants or oppressors over the choirs below them. Their ranking and authority protect them from being subject to any tyranny and oppression, whether on earth or in Heaven.[28] Thus they have an extraordinary elevation in the duties that have been given them and complete freedom in the discharge of those duties.[29]

The Fourth Salutation:
For the Grace to Overcome Unruly Passions

If you are like many people, when you hear the word "passion," you probably picture a young couple deeply in love with each other. That is partly true, according to the popular definition of the word. Passion frequently is used in the context of sexual attraction and relationships, and we are inundated with it in advertisements, movies, television shows, books, and even in conversations. We are led to believe that physically-attractive persons should evoke passion in our hearts and that, if we become physically attractive, we will evoke passion in the hearts of others, but this passion is born of lust or vanity and not genuine love. Certain makeup, perfume, cologne, clothing, or physiques will help us achieve that goal. Passion is something we are encouraged to pursue for the sake of sensual pleasure or self-image. This kind of passion is superficial and can be damaging to our souls.

But passion also can refer to a burning desire to fulfill one's dreams. For example, an artist who pursues his trade relentlessly and with great devotion is considered passionate. Or an avid history buff might be considered as having a passion for history. A future aviator can be passionate about learning to fly an airplane and perhaps someday become an airline pilot. A faithful Catholic can be passionate about following the teachings of the Church so as to please God in all things.

We can — and should — be passionate in our love for God, and we should be passionate about following His commandments. In these contexts, passion is a form of motivation that draws us toward that which we perceive as good or in some way fulfills a need within us.

What are passions, and where do they come from? The *Catechism of the Catholic Church* gives a great definition for us to consider:

> The term "passions" belongs to the Christian patrimony. Feelings or passions are emotions or movements of the sensitive appetite that incline us to act or not to act in regard to something felt or imagined to be good or evil.[30]

The *Catechism* goes on to examine the importance of passions in our human nature:

> The passions are natural components of the human psyche; they form the passageway and ensure the

connection between the life of the senses and the life of the mind. Our Lord called man's heart the source from which the passions spring.[31]

In and of themselves, passions are neither good nor evil because they are a normal human emotion and part of who we are. It is how we manage them that makes the difference. Passions can be enhanced by virtues or perverted by vices, depending on how we allow them to engage our will or inspire our souls. When we allow evil passions to take over our minds and hearts, they become unruly and separate us from God's grace.

Saint Paul warned the Galatians about such passions:

> Live by the Spirit, I say, and do not gratify the desires of the flesh. For what the flesh desires is opposed to the Spirit, and what the Spirit desires is opposed to the flesh; for these are opposed to each other, to prevent you from doing what you want. But if you are led by the Spirit, you are not subject to the law. Now the works of the flesh are obvious: fornication, impurity, licentiousness, idolatry, sorcery, enmities, strife, jealousy, anger, quarrels, dissensions, factions, envy, drunkenness, carousing, and things like these. I am warning you, as I warned you before: those who do such things will not inherit the kingdom of God (Gal 5:16–21).

The Apostle's warning does not mince words. If we allow unruly passions to overcome us, we forfeit eternity. And so the Church cautions us to be prudent in dealing with what it calls the "principal passions" — love, hatred, desire, fear, joy, sadness, and anger.[32] Each of these can be used for good as in hatred toward Satan and anger over injustice, or evil as in succumbing to immoral drives.

Examining the Influence of Impurity

You may have heard the adage "Sex sells." Unfortunately, it is indeed effective because it appeals to a spontaneous and base drive within us. We need only to glance at a lewd image and our senses are piqued in such a way that we are prone to make decisions we might not otherwise. Entertainers, moviemakers, publishers, and advertisers all know that.

In an article that appeared in *Business News Daily*, the author explains that companies use sexually-charged content in their campaigns because it is effective and memorable. Grabbing viewers' and potential buyers' attention is half the battle in selling any product or service. The article quotes Tom Reichert, researcher and former head of the University of Georgia Department of Advertising and Public Relations: "Advertisers use sex because it can be very effective. Sex sells because it attracts attention. People are hardwired to notice sexually relevant information, so ads with sexual content get noticed."[33]

This hardwiring is what makes us vulnerable to impurity, and Satan knows that. The Church tells us that our sexuality affects "all aspects of the human person in the unity of his body and soul."[34] Therefore, Satan will use every trick up his sleeve to tempt us toward impurity through our minds, hearts, and bodies. We are, in essence, easy targets for him because we are sensual in nature. It is as if he were running a relentless ad campaign to lure us into impurity, a pervasive evil that manifests itself in sexual immorality.

In the Sermon on the Mount, our Lord gave us the eight Beatitudes, the sixth of which lauds the pure of heart and promises that they will see God. In this passage, Jesus is pointing out that the key to resisting impurity and avoiding eternal punishment is to keep our hearts pure in the first place. That may sound simple, but it is more complicated than you think. We can commit sins of impurity without taking any actions or even being aware of it. Sin is not always something we do; it often is something we merely think even when our thoughts are fleeting and not deliberate:

> You have heard that it was said, "You shall not commit adultery." But I say to you that everyone who looks at a woman with lust has already committed adultery with her in her heart. If your right eye causes

> you to sin, tear it out and throw it away; it is better
> for you to lose one of your members than for your
> whole body to be thrown into hell. And if your right
> hand causes you to sin, cut it off and throw it away;
> it is better for you to lose one of your members than
> for your whole body to go into hell (Mt 5:27–30).

Our Lord warns us to be constantly on guard of what we allow ourselves to be exposed to or think about, thus avoiding any near occasion of sin. Many people mistakenly believe that they can be around indecent entertainment or conversation and not be affected. He encourages us to go to the extreme to resist impurity by entirely cutting out of our lives whatever might lead us astray, no matter the cost (see Mt 18:19). If we do that, St. James wrote in his letter, we will be rewarded in Heaven:

> Blessed is anyone who endures temptation. Such a
> one has stood the test and will receive the crown
> of life that the Lord has promised to those who
> love him. No one, when tempted, should say, "I
> am being tempted by God"; for God cannot be
> tempted by evil and he himself tempts no one. But
> one is tempted by one's own desire, being lured and
> enticed by it; then, when that desire has conceived,
> it gives birth to sin, and that sin, when it is fully
> grown, gives birth to death. Do not be deceived,
> my beloved (Jas 1:12–16).

Facing Your Personal Challenges

When I think about resisting impurity, I immediately think of St. Maria Goretti. She is a great inspiration to me, not only because she is my daughter's Confirmation saint, but because I find her story remarkable.

Maria Goretti (known as Marietta to friends and family) lived in Ancona, Italy, in the late 1800s with her family of peasant farmers. Her father died when she was 10 years old, and so she had to tend to the house and younger children while her mother worked in the fields to support the family. They shared living space above an old barn with the Serenelli family, who had a son named Alessandro who was nearly 10 years older than Maria. Maria saw him as a brother, but he thought differently about her and made continuous sexual advances toward her, threatening to kill her if she told anyone about it.

On July 5, 1902, Maria was alone in the house when Alessandro came back there from the fields. He dragged her inside and tried to force himself upon her, but she resisted fiercely, the entire time pleading with Alessandro not to commit this terrible sin. Out of anger and frustration, he stabbed her and fled. Maria was taken to hospital but died the next day. Before she died, she forgave Alessandro "for the love of Jesus."

Alessandro was sentenced to 30 years in prison and initially was unrepentant of the evil he had done. Then one night, he had a dream in which Maria appeared to him and offered him lilies. From then on he was a completely changed man and, upon release, went immediately to Maria's mother to ask her forgiveness. He was present at Maria's canonization in 1950.[35]

Maria understood the importance of remaining pure, and she resisted impurity with fatal consequences. She likely would not have been condemned in the opinions of others because of her precarious situation in that moment. But she did not care about the opinions of human beings; she cared about the opinion of God.

What a striking contrast to those of us who disregard lewd gestures and conversations or participate in impure entertainment and events because it is too much of a bother to counter or avoid them. We excuse ourselves for giving into a moment of passion because we "just couldn't help it." But we *can* help it! Not only that, but we *must* help it, and with the grace of God and the intercession of the Dominions, we can.

Questions for Reflection

- What is my genuine attitude toward impure language, comments, or entertainment?
- What is my greatest weakness in trying to resist impurity?
- When or how am I most vulnerable?
- What concrete actions can I take when faced with these situations?

Resolutions

Read again the Gospel of Matthew 5:27–30. Make a copy of it, print it out, and keep it in a place that is visible to you daily. Ask our Lord for help in letting this passage sink deeply into your mind and heart.

Invoking the Dominions

O Holy Dominions,

You emanate perfect humility despite your high place in Heaven. What a great honor it must be to be so close to God that you become as though you were a physical throne for Him! Your position in Heaven allows you to be strengthened by God in a direct way, making you a symbol of His strength. You demonstrate stability and power and have a knowledge of the divine that I cannot comprehend. It would seem, by human standards, that you would have a right to be prideful, but you are not.

Teach me how to have holy stewardship of my body and governance of my mind. Pray for me to have the strength to stop my unruly passions from becoming tyrants over my thoughts and actions. Help me to be constantly vigilant for situations that might tempt me toward impurity and show me how to root them out of my life completely. Intercede for me in my weakness; help me to resist impurity at all costs.

Amen.

DAY 5

Invoking the Choir of Virtues
Resist Gluttony

Learning from God's Messengers:
The Choir of Virtues

Regarding the Orders of Angels, St. Thomas Aquinas wrote, "This diversity of order arises from the diversity of offices and actions, as appears in one city where there are different orders according to the different actions; for there is one order of those who judge, and another of those who fight, and another of those who labor in the fields, and so forth."[36] Pseudo-Dionysius, the fifth- or sixth-century philosophical theologian and mystic, believed that the names of the various orders signify the spiritual perfections they symbolize.

In contrast, Pope St. Gregory I believed that the names of the Choirs of Angels symbolize the duties they administer. For example, the Choir of Angels are messengers, the Powers defeat earthly powers, and the Principalities rule over those in their charge.[37] In the writings of others who study angels, it seems to be a combination of the two.

Given this, where did the Choir of Virtues get their name? The Greek word used to refer to the virtues is the word from which the English adjective "dynamic" is derived. From that we get the nouns "dynamo" and "dynamite," both of which imply force or energy. Perhaps, then, we could think of the Virtues as the dynamos of the Choirs of Angels!

The word "virtue" comes from Latin, and we most commonly associate it with moral qualities and sometimes with physical qualities. For example, we think of a specific virtue,

such as humility. Or we may think of a virtuous woman, refer-
ring to her purity and devotedness to God. In less common
usage, we might refer to the virtues of a medicinal herb in
reference to its ability to heal the body. Virtues also could be
understood as miracles or mighty works.[38]

We can learn much about virtue from St. Peter. In his
letters, he wrote to the persecuted Christians scattered
throughout Asia Minor. He was concerned for both their
physical and spiritual welfare and used his letters to guide
them through their trials:

> For this very reason, you must make every effort
> to support your faith with goodness, and goodness
> with knowledge, and knowledge with self-control,
> and self-control with endurance, and endurance
> with godliness, and godliness with mutual affection,
> and mutual affection with love. For if these things
> are yours and are increasing among you, they keep
> you from being ineffective and unfruitful in the
> knowledge of our Lord Jesus Christ (2 Peter 1:5–8).

In essence, Peter is talking about the virtues and living a virtuous life. One could say that Peter's words also refer to the
Choir of Virtues and the example they set for us, which defines
both their name and the duties they administer. Additionally,
the name "virtues" symbolize their participation in divine virtue because of their closeness to God.

Who Are the Virtues?

The Virtues are ranked in the second hierarchy of angels along
with the Dominions and Powers because of their similarity in
tasks and character. All three choirs share in a common government or disposition, giving them the authority to govern
the lower Choirs of Angels as well as humans. According to St.
Thomas Aquinas, the name "virtues" represents a certain virile
and immovable strength in terms of their being, duties, and
the divine gifts they receive. They fearlessly carry out God's
requests, which also implies a strength of mind. While the
Dominions appoint what needs to be done, the Virtues carry

it out. They are given the responsibility of working miracles and governing, or influencing, human activity.[39]

In *The Holy Angels,* Fr. O'Connell wrote that the Virtues are "those blessed spirits whom God commonly employs for the working of signs and miracles" or for whatever is outside the regular order of events established by God.[40] This includes the preservation and government of humanity. Although we may not recognize their activity, the Virtues are frequently at work, intervening and interceding on our behalf. We might not even be aware that anything supernatural has happened and brush it aside as coincidence or something caused by ourselves or other human beings. But be assured that in these circumstances, the Virtues have been at work in your life.

The Fifth Salutation:
For Perseverance Against Evil and
Falling into Temptation

In the third salutation of the Chaplet of St. Michael, we invoke the Choir of Virtues for preservation from evil and falling into temptation. We are asking them to block the actions of the evil one in our lives and to help us to be strong against all temptation. Even more, we are asking them to prevent us from falling into temptation in the first place! With the strength of mind they've been endowed with according to their office, the Virtues are the perfect choir to invoke for this purpose.

Because of original sin, we are prone to temptation in our lives. We generally think of temptation in terms of more serious sins such as theft, adultery, or even murder. Satan would love it if we committed those sins, but he also would like us to sin in less obvious ways. Whether it be slandering someone we don't like or viewing lewd content on the television or computer, we are continuously bombarded by the near occasion of sin. Much of the time, we aren't even aware of the demons' activity until after we have committed the sin. Sometimes we don't detect it at all.

None of us are immune from temptation, no matter how ardent our prayer life or frequently we receive the Sacraments. Our Lord is aware of that, and so He even permitted Satan to tempt Him to set an example for us. Jesus' custom was to go to a secluded place and pray to His Father before a turning point in His ministry. After His Baptism by St. John the Baptist and before He gave the Sermon on the Mount, which marked the beginning of His public ministry, He went alone into the desert and fasted for 40 days and 40 nights, spending the time in prayer and contemplation. At the end of the 40 days, Satan came before Him and tempted Him with nourishment, power, and wealth. He knew that Jesus' human body was weak from lack of food, which can also weaken a person's mind and spirit. With each temptation, he dared our Lord to use His divine power to obtain bread (or things of the flesh), power, and worldly recognition (or pride). Each time, Jesus rebuked Satan, declaring that nothing matters more than God and living in His grace.

With this example, Jesus is showing us how vulnerable we are and how desperate Satan is to stop us from progressing in our pursuit of spiritual perfection. He understands how difficult it can be to resist the evil one's temptations, so He sends us the Virtues to help us along the way.

Examining the Influence of Gluttony

Satan first tempted Jesus with bread because he knows that it is in a sense a first line of defense for an aspiring Christian. Because of our human nature, it is difficult to resist seeking bodily pleasures since we need them to some degree. We cannot survive without food, drink, sleep, or affection, for example. Without procreation, our species would not survive. If we do not care for our bodies, we will become ill or even die. While on earth, Jesus ate, drank, slept, and enjoyed the friendship of others because He was fully human. Fulfilling our bodily needs is not sinful in and of itself; it becomes problematic when we overindulge, particularly when it comes to eating or drinking too much. When we do that, we are committing the sin of gluttony, which is one of the seven cardinal sins. Along with pride, avarice, envy, wrath, lust, and sloth (acedia), gluttony is considered a capital sin because it engenders other sins. By allowing Himself to be tempted with bread, Jesus is showing us that ordering our bodily appetites is paramount to resisting other types of sin. Having control of our bodily impulses strengthens us against other sinful impulses.

Saint John Vianney referred to gluttony as "shameful" because it degrades the human person. In one of his homilies on gluttony, he said:

> See, it puts us below the brutes: the animals never drink more than to satisfy their thirst: they content themselves with eating enough; and we, when we have satisfied our appetite, when our body can bear no more, we still have recourse to all sorts of little delicacies; we take wine and liquors to repletion! Is it not pitiful?[41]

He went on to caution us that we risk the fires of hell should we die and face particular judgment in that state:

> If death were to surprise us in this state, my children, we should not have time to recollect ourselves; we should fall in that state into the hands of the good God. What a misfortune, my children! How our soul would be surprised! How it would be astonished! We should shudder with horror at seeing the lost who are in Hell. ... Do not let us be led by our appetite; we shall ruin our health; we shall lose our soul.

Saint Paul also sounded the alarm in reference to gluttony. In his Letter to the Galatians, he explained that living by the flesh deters us from living by the Spirit. When we live by the flesh, we make our bodies into gods, giving them control over us by dictating our thoughts and behavior. We allow them to govern us instead of the opposite. On the other hand, when we live in the Spirit, we follow His promptings to follow the will and commandments of God in all things.

In his letter, Paul writes of his concerns for the young Christian community he had founded there. While he was away from them, the Galatians fell under the influence of misdirected missionaries and had become lax in the principles he had taught them. Thus, things were falling apart and the community needed redirection. He admonishes them for living by the flesh and implores them to instead live by the Spirit.

> Live by the Spirit, I say, and do not gratify the desires of the flesh. For what the flesh desires is opposed to the Spirit, and what the Spirit desires is opposed to the flesh; for these are opposed to each other, to prevent you from doing what you want. But if you are led by the Spirit, you are not subject to the law. Now the works of the flesh are obvious: fornication, impurity, licentiousness, idolatry, sorcery, enmities, strife, jealousy, anger, quarrels, dissensions, factions, envy, drunkenness, carousing, and things like these. I am warning you, as I warned you before: those who do such things will not inherit the kingdom of God (Gal. 5:16–21).

Living by the Spirit will help us to see that our bodies are truly a gift from God and so we should treat them as such. They have been given to us to be used for the greater glory of God and the building of His Kingdom, not for pursuit of our own selfish desires. Therefore, we are called to treat them with respect and care because they really don't belong to us — they belong to our Heavenly Father, just as all of creation belongs to Him.

Facing Your Personal Challenges

Sometimes it seems that when we think we are most strong, we are most weak. We like to believe that we are capable of handling things on our own, able to choose for ourselves and govern our own lives. That could not be further from the truth. In his Letter to the Corinthians, Paul warned them against thinking they were immune from temptation and waywardness:

> So, if you think you are standing, watch out that you do not fall. No testing has overtaken you that is not common to everyone. God is faithful, and he

will not let you be tested beyond your strength, but with the testing he will also provide the way out so that you may be able to endure it (1 Cor 10:12–13).

Paul reminds the Colossians — and us — that we must expect temptation and be wary of falling into it. Satan most surely will do all in his power to coerce us and draw us into sin, particularly the capital sins. God will allow us to be tempted, but also will give us the strength and grace we need to resist it if we depend on Him.

An old potato chip commercial bore the catchphrase "Betcha can't each just one!" The potato chip company plays on our senses, urging us to mentally savor the taste and crunch of the chips, and trying to convince us that the chips are so good that we will have to eat the whole bag to be satisfied. The hard and fast truth is that the company is tempting us to gluttony by eating an entire bag of chips that are not nourishing and that our bodies (and our waistlines) do not need.

The principle of this simple example is applied countless times and in countless ways in our day-to-day living. Gluttony is an insidious evil that weaves its way into our lives under the auspices of innocent pleasure and even need. Once we develop the propensity for gluttony, it is easier to develop the propensity for greed, lust, and a host of other sins.

Questions for Reflection

- What is my attitude toward food and drink?
- Do I have a firm stopping point, or do I tend to overindulge?
- Are there certain foods or drinks that I am especially weak in resisting?
- What are my triggers for gluttony (emotions, situations, people, etc.)?

Resolutions

Make a list of the types of foods, drinks, and situations that most tempt you to gluttony. Ask yourself why each of them makes it hard to resist overindulging. Then take the list into prayer and offer it to our Lord, asking Him for the strength and grace to be vigilant and resistant to gluttony.

Invoking the Virtues

O, Holy Virtues,

You are the dynamos of the Choirs of Angels! You have been given the authority to govern the lower choirs as well as human beings. You have been charged with carrying out God's will, and for this you have been gifted with virility and immovable strength of both celestial body and mind. You have been given divine gifts that no other choir has been given. With your gifts, you carry out God's holy will. With your gifts, you are well suited to assist me in resisting the sin of gluttony.

Because of your characteristics and position in the angelic hierarchy, God often chooses you to work signs and miracles in Heaven and on earth. You are constantly at work, interceding on behalf of all humanity and working miracles in our lives. You watch over me with great care, performing miracles of which I am seldom aware or that my skepticism obstructs me from believing in. This causes me to be ungrateful for all that you do for and around me. Please help me to be truly grateful for all that you are and do for me.

By the intercession of St. Michael and the celestial Choir of Virtues, may the Lord preserve me from evil and falling into temptation.

Amen.

DAY 6

Invoking the Choir of Powers
Resist Avarice

Learning from God's Messengers:
The Choir of Powers

Aside from St. Paul's Letter to the Colossians, Scripture does not specifically mention the Choir of Powers. In his letter (cited previously in Day 3), the Apostle refers to the Powers only in terms of their relationship to our Lord as King of all creation:

> He is the image of the invisible God, the firstborn of all creation; for in him all things in heaven and on earth were created, things visible and invisible, whether thrones or dominions or rulers or powers — all things have been created through him and for him. He himself is before all things, and in him all things hold together (Col 1:15–17).

Again, in his Letter to the Ephesians, Paul lists the Powers in relation to Christ's power and position:

> God put this power to work in Christ when he raised him from the dead and seated him at his right hand in the heavenly places, far above all rule and authority and power and dominion, and above every name that is named, not only in this age but also in the age to come. And he has put all things under his feet and has made him the head over all things for the church, which is his body, the fullness of him who fills all in all (Eph 1:20–23).

In these brief mentions lies a small clue to the character of the Choir of Powers. We could surmise that the Powers are a choir of great strength because Paul makes it a point to say that Christ is so great that He is even greater than they. This comparison suggests that the Powers are a formidable opponent in spiritual battle and hold a prominent position in the celestial hierarchy.

Later in the letter, Paul counsels the Ephesians to be strengthened in God and courageous against evil forces. It is as if he is exhorting them to be like the Powers:

> Finally, be strong in the Lord and in the strength of his power. Put on the whole armor of God, so that you may be able to stand against the wiles of the devil. For our struggle is not against enemies of blood and flesh, but against the rulers, against the authorities, against the cosmic powers of this present darkness, against the spiritual forces of evil in the heavenly places. Therefore, take up the whole armor of God, so that you may be able to withstand on that evil day, and having done everything, to stand firm. Stand therefore, and fasten the belt of truth around your waist, and put on the breastplate of righteousness. As shoes for your feet put on whatever will make you ready to proclaim the gospel of peace. With all of these, take the shield of faith, with which you will be able to quench all the flaming arrows of the evil one. Take the helmet of salvation, and the sword of the Spirit, which is the word of God (Eph 6:10–17).

In our struggle against demonic influence and our tendency toward sinfulness, we would do well to invoke the Choir of Powers. Through their intercession and under their protection, we will be able to "put on the armor of God" and stand firm against evil.

Who Are the Powers?

Just as the name of each of the Choirs of Angels signifies their likeness to God and participation in his grace and attributes, the name "powers" is reflective of the almighty power of God. Saint Thomas Aquinas explained that the name "power" points out a kind of order, and that whoever resists the power of the Powers also resists the power of God. Given their position in the angelic hierarchy, the Powers are charged with the responsibility to maintain a kind of order according to the will of God, and to regulate the actions and responsibilities of those beneath them. It is up to them to decide what needs to be done and to see that it is accomplished.[42]

Also reflective of their name, the Powers hold the office of planning and directing the spiritual battle between humans and demons. They subvert the demons' designs and are especially effective in subduing their efforts. Because of the Powers' character and position in the angelic hierarchy, Satan and his minions are obligated to obey them. And so, the Powers have the direct ability to command, constrain, and even fetter the demons.[43]

In the Book of Daniel, three young men were thrown into the fiery furnace by King Nebuchadnezzar because they refused to fall down and worship the king's golden idol. Shadrach, Meshach, and Abednego walked freely among the flames, singing hymns, praising the Lord, and proclaiming His faithfulness to those who follow His commandments. Amid their praises they called upon the angels, and in particular the Powers, to uphold them in their suffering and defeat the evil that surrounded them:

> Bless the Lord, you angels of the Lord;
> sing praise to him and highly exalt him forever.
> Bless the Lord, all you waters above the heavens;
> sing praise to him and highly exalt him forever.
> Bless the Lord, all you powers of the Lord;
> sing praise to him and highly exalt him forever
> (Dan 3:59–61).

King Nebuchadnezzar was astounded to hear the young men singing and went to see for himself what was happening. When he peered into the furnace, he saw four unharmed men walking amid the flames, with the fourth having "the appearance of a god." Clearly the fourth figure in the furnace was an angel sent to rescue Shadrach, Meshach, and Abednego. Could it have been one of the Powers? This cannot be determined with certainty, but it is a good possibility.

The Sixth Salutation:
For Protection Against the Snares and
Temptations of the Devil

Because of original sin, the devil has obtained a dominant influence over human beings despite God having given us free will. Our wounded nature inclines us toward evil and makes us vulnerable to Satan's lies and trickery. This causes our lives to be a continual battle of good versus evil, as we must relentlessly fight against the demons' aggression.[44] According to *Gaudium et Spes*:

> For a monumental struggle against the powers of darkness pervades the whole history of man. The battle was joined from the very origins of the world and will continue until the last day, as the Lord has attested. Caught in this conflict, man is obliged to wrestle constantly if he is to cling to what is good, nor can he achieve his own integrity without great efforts and the help of God's grace.[45]

Although we desire to do what is good, our nature is wounded and predisposes us to error and the influence of the evil one. Except for the Blessed Virgin Mary, no human being is free of this struggle, including the greatest of saints and even the Doctors of the Church. Saint Paul wrote frankly about his weakness and of his struggle with evil and temptation in his Letter to the Romans. He understood that, even though our Lord had commissioned him to preach the Good News, he was "of the flesh," because of original sin and his own human weakness. He knew what God expected of him, and yet he often acted against God's will and his own desire to do what was right. He wrote, "For I do not do the good I want, but the evil I do not want is what I do. Now if I do what I do not want, it is no longer I that do it, but sin that dwells within me."[46]

Saint Paul could have written this about all of us. Deep in our hearts, we know what is evil or spiritually dangerous. Yet we do it anyway because we ignore the stirrings of our hearts and allow ourselves to be tricked or coerced by the devil to do what is sinful. We remain in a constant state of conflict — sometimes stronger, sometimes milder — as we stand between the powers of hell and the powers of Heaven. Satan knows this and will do all he can to deceive us and trap us into committing sin. Jesus referred to Satan as the "prince" or "ruler" of this world, cautioning us to always strive to avoid the darkness and become children of the light who walk in God's ways (see Jn 12:31–36).

According to *Gaudium et Spes*, this dramatic struggle between good and evil, light and darkness, causes us to be split within ourselves, and keeps us as if bound in chains.[47] The *Catechism* refers to Satan as "a murderer from the beginning ... a liar and the father of lies ... the deceiver of the whole world" who brought sin and death into the world.[48] We cannot fight Satan and his demons on our own, but with God's help we can stand strong against him and defend ourselves from his hatred, cunning, and deception. God is our loving Father, Savior, and Paraclete who wants nothing more than to provide all that is best for us and to welcome us into eternity at the end of our lives. He wants us to be children of the light and will provide us with the means to defend ourselves in the battle against evil.

One means He already has provided is the Choir of Powers. Therefore, we invoke the Powers for protection against the snares and temptations of the devil as they are charged with the responsibility to maintain order according to God's will. They direct the battle between demons and humans and will direct our individual battle with Satan if we invoke and entrust ourselves to their safekeeping.

Examining the Influence of Avarice

Those who live in developed countries — such as the United States — have become accustomed to being surrounded by many possessions. Granted, there are exceptions, but for the most part we are used to having modern conveniences at our disposal, and plenty of them. It is interesting, and perhaps alarming, that one modern convenience sparks a need for another, and another, and so on.

For example, consider the television. When it was invented, it was deemed better than radio since it brought both audio and video into people's homes and so everyone wanted one. The first television offered black-and-white images, but once the color television was invented, people hurried to get one because color was deemed better than black-and-white. It was the same when the flat-screen television was invented; everyone wanted one because it was deemed better than the box-style model. Then came HDTV (high-density TV), then large-screen, and then the "smart" television, and so on. Each new advancement created a new desire to obtain it. We did not absolutely need it; we just wanted it. This is not to say that every person who purchases an updated model of the television (or any other device) is necessarily guilty of avarice. It merely points out how easy it is to want things just for the sake of having them when they really aren't necessary for our spiritual or physical well-being. It is, in essence, a mild form of avarice.

Some may think that only those who spend their lives accumulating wealth and possessions are greedy. In truth, they are not the only ones who succumb to the sin of avarice. Indeed, we are all vulnerable even if we own very little. The Letter to the Hebrews warns us against getting caught up in materialism: "Keep your lives free from the love of money and be content with what you have; for he has said, 'I will never leave you or forsake you'" (Heb 13:5). Note that the passage does not warn against the love of large quantities of money. Rather, it warns against the love of money at all. Just as with the television example in the previous paragraph, the accumulation of money sparks the need for a greater accumulation of money. No matter how much we have in the bank, no matter how rich we become, we continue to want more. We compare ourselves to others and falsely assume that we do not measure up because we own less than they do. The more we have, the more we want, and we forget that it is not about what we want, but rather what God wants for us.

Building up material things — not just money but also clothes, jewelry, devices, and the like — makes us feel more worthy and important. But to God, we are immeasurably worthy and important even if we were penniless and did not own a single thing. In fact, that is how He brought us into this world! He loves us for who we are and has promised in a multitude of ways that He will never forsake us.

Facing Your Personal Challenges

After the Transfiguration on Mount Tabor, Jesus and His disciples went to Capernaum in Galilee and then to the region of Judea across the Jordan River. All the while He taught the crowds about the Kingdom of God. As He taught, a rich young man approached Him, wanting to know how to secure His entrance into Heaven. The dialogue between our Lord and the young man tells us much about the sin of avarice and how to avoid it.

> Then someone came to him and said, "Teacher, what good deed must I do to have eternal life?" And he said to him, "Why do you ask me about what is good? There is only one who is good. If you wish to enter into life, keep the commandments." He said to him, "Which ones?" And Jesus said, "You shall not murder; You shall not commit adultery; You shall not steal; You shall not bear false witness; Honor your father and mother; also, You shall love your neighbor as yourself." The young man said to him, "I have kept all these; what do I still lack?" Jesus said to him, "If you wish to be perfect, go, sell your possessions, and give the money to the poor, and you will have treasure in heaven; then come, follow me." When the young man heard this word,

he went away grieving, for he had many possessions
(Mt 19:16–22).

This story makes me wonder whether I could give
everything away in pursuit of eternity. I, like many people, consider myself a good person because I keep the commandments,
receive the Sacraments, and pray daily. Isn't that enough to
get me into Heaven? Quite frankly, our Lord says it is not.
I may not have riches to give away, but I have things that I
consider important and that keep me from avoiding the snares
and temptations of the devil. I have a computer, cellphone,
television, and tablet. They can help me to do great good in
the world, but they also can distract me from doing the work
God has assigned to me. They even can lead me into sinful
entertainment. Completely abandoning them to follow Jesus
would be extremely difficult. Like the rich young man, I fear
I may walk away from our Lord grieving because I could not
give them up for His sake.

Questions for Reflection

- Am I satisfied simply with following the
  commandments? What more could I do?

- Which of my possessions do I most cherish?
  Why do I cherish them?

- Would I be able to surrender them to follow Jesus?

Resolutions

Make a general list of your possessions, including any mon-
etary accumulation. Look over the list. Assess each item
and its meaning in your life; both physically and spiritually.
Thank God for them and surrender them to our Lord, asking
Him to make them holy and guide you in your use of them.
Then spiritually "give" them to Him without reserve.

Invoking the Powers

O Holy Powers,

You are a choir of great strength, a formidable opponent in spiritual battle. Saint Paul used you as a measure of Christ's greatness, thus placing you in a prominent position in the celestial hierarchy. He used you as an example of what the Ephesians — and all disciples of Christ — should be like. Like you, I must put on the armor of God so that I may be able to stand against Satan's wiles. Like you, I must fasten the belt of truth around my waist, put on the breastplate of righteousness, and be ready to proclaim the Gospel to all. Like you, I must take up the shield of faith that will guard me against the flaming arrows of the evil one. Finally, I must take up the helmet of salvation and the sword of the Spirit, which is the word of God.

The evil one is strong and cunning, and my fallen nature makes it difficult for me to fight against him. I am constantly caught in the struggle between good and evil, light and darkness. I want to walk in the light but so often find myself fumbling in the dark. God has given you the strength and responsibility to assist and protect me in this battle. May I daily be reminded to call on you in my moments of weakness.

By the intercession of St. Michael and the celestial Choir of Powers, may the Lord protect my soul against the snares and temptations of the devil.

Amen.

DAY 7

Invoking the Choir of Principalities
Resist Wrath

Learning from God's Messengers:
The Choir of Principalities

In secular terms, a principality is a state, territory, or jurisdiction of a prince. In the course of history, principalities might have been part of a larger entity, like an empire. In many cases, the title given to the ruler of such a state or territory was "principality." In modern times, we sometimes see other figures of responsibility referred to as the principality, like a principal of a school, for example.

When we think of princes and territories, we might think about the princes of medieval times, who were given charge over a certain area of the kingdom. Princes could inherit their own castles and estates, and the oldest prince in a family was heir to his father's throne. Princes were trained in the art of warfare from an early age, becoming masters of swordsmanship and other assorted weapons. A prince's main responsibility was to ensure the sovereignty of his state and the well-being of his tenants. Tenants could live and work on the prince's land, but in return they paid rent and were required to give the prince a certain percentage of their earnings and crops.[49] Likely you are familiar with stories of princes who treated their tenants with cruelty, charged far more rent and taxes than deserved, or made other unjust rules for their territories. In its purest form, the feudal system was meant to be beneficial to everyone by providing a livelihood and protection for all the people.

We might then think of the Heavenly Kingdom as a puri-
fied form of an earthly kingdom, with the angelic Principalities
fulfilling a similar role as the human principalities. The biggest
difference is that the Principalities give rather than receive.
They collect no goods, rent, or taxes, but instead offer divine
protection and guidance. Their reward is in knowing that they
are carrying out the will of God.

During the Babylonian exile of the Israelites and after
the fall of Babylon to Persia, the prophet Daniel went into a
period of mourning over yet another travesty in the history of
his people. For three weeks, he prayed, lamented, abstained
from meat and wine, and ate meagerly. As he stood one day
on the bank of the Tigris River, he was approached by a man
clothed in linen with a belt of gold around his waist and his
body appearing like beryl (a precious gem). His face was like
lightning, his eyes like flaming torches, his arms and legs were
like the gleam of burnished bronze. His voice was so powerful
that it sounded like the roar of a multitude. No one else saw
the vision, and Daniel was frightened to the point of becoming
faint. When the man began speaking, Daniel fell face to the
ground in a trance. However, the man who stood before him
was not a human being, but rather a celestial being — a Principality and member of the third hierarchy of angels, along with
the Archangels and Angels.

The being touched Daniel's shoulder and lifted him to his
hands and knees. He then spoke to the beleaguered prophet:

> "Daniel, greatly beloved, pay attention to the words
> that I am going to speak to you. Stand on your feet,
> for I have now been sent to you." So while he was
> speaking this word to me, I stood up trembling.
> He said to me, "Do not fear, Daniel, for from the
> first day that you set your mind to gain understand-
> ing and to humble yourself before your God, your
> words have been heard, and I have come because of
> your words. But the prince of the kingdom of Persia
> opposed me twenty-one days. So Michael, one of
> the chief princes, came to help me, and I left him

there with the prince of the kingdom of Persia, and have come to help you understand what is to happen to your people at the end of days. For there is a further vision for those days" (Dan 10:10–14).

The angel's words caused great anguish in Daniel's heart and deepened his fear to the point of becoming unable to breathe. He was convinced that he was too weak to endure the future that the angel predicted. The angel again touched Daniel and offered him words of reassurance:

> Again one in human form touched me and strengthened me. He said, "Do not fear, greatly beloved, you are safe. Be strong and courageous!" When he spoke to me, I was strengthened and said, "Let my lord speak, for you have strengthened me." Then he said, "Do you know why I have come to you? Now I must return to fight against the prince of Persia, and when I am through with him, the prince of Greece will come. But I am to tell you what is inscribed in the book of truth. There is no one with me who contends against these princes except Michael, your prince" (Dan 10:18–21).

As suggested by the Scripture narrative, the Principalities are involved in the care of nations, kingdoms, and communities. In the scene with Daniel, the principality came to contend with the demonic princes of Persia and Greece whose only goal was to annihilate God's people.

Who Are the Principalities?

The name "principality" comes from the Latin word *principari*, meaning to make a beginning, be the first to lead forward, point out the way, direct, or legislate. By his supremacy and strength, God holds universal dominion and sets down laws that order all things in anticipation of their destiny. As we find in the Book of Proverbs, "By me kings reign, and rulers decree what is just; by me rulers rule, and nobles, all who govern rightly" (Prov 8:15–16). This attribute of God is typified by the Choir of

Principalities, and they are commissioned to constantly praise God for His wisdom in ruling and legislating the whole of creation.[50]

According to St. Thomas Aquinas, the name "principality" denotes "one who leads in a sacred order." They are thus named because they are the leading choir in the last hierarchy of angels:

> The execution of the angelic ministrations consists in announcing Divine things. Now in the execution of any action there are beginners and leaders; as in singing, the precentors; and in war, generals and officers; this belongs to the "Principalities." There are others who simply execute what is to be done; and these are the "Angels." Others hold a middle place; and these are the "Archangels," as above explained.[51]

The Principalities are the princes of the angels who symbolize God's *princeliness* and authoritativeness. They are viewed as guardians of governments, kingdoms, nations, and communities as well as of those who rule and govern them. They are part of the "ring of salvation," as the third hierarchy is called, and look after the spiritual life of the Church as well as the redemption of mankind.[52] They have authority over the Archangels and Angels, and impart God's will to them. Just as a military general commands and plans the operations of troops in the field, so too the Principalities plan (according to God's will) and command the operations of the angelic hierarchy in the field of battle against Satan.

In Scripture and in various devotions, St. Michael and also St. Gabriel are referred to as heavenly princes, despite also being clearly named as Archangels. This is true of the opening example of this chapter taken from the Book of Daniel. The principality who appeared to Daniel told him, "So Michael, one of the chief princes, came to help me." How can Michael be both a Prince (Principality) and an Archangel? It is less confusing when we understand that the choirs and hierarchies of angels are a continuum, rather than a set of concrete divisions.

In his book *The Angels in Catholic Teaching and Tradition*, Fr. Pascal Parente quotes Plato: "The progression of beings are completed through similitude. However, the terminations of the higher orders are united to the beginnings of the second orders ... and thus all things are in continuity with each other." In this way, St. Michael can be both an Archangel and a heavenly Prince.

In his love and providence, God has formed the Choir of Principalities for our sakes and as a reflection of His own divine authority. As Pseudo-Dionysius wrote:

> The name of celestial Principalities signifies their Godlike princeliness and authoritativeness in an order which is holy and most fitting to the princely powers, and that they are wholly turned towards the Prince of princes, and lead others in princely fashion. They are formed, as far as creatures can be, in the likeness of the Source of principality and reveal Its transcendent order by the good order of the princely powers.[53]

The Seventh Salutation:
For a True Spirit of Obedience

Within the Choir of Principalities, we clearly see the polar opposites of obedience. On the one hand, we see princes who have valiantly followed the commands of their Divine Prince, sometimes referred to as the "good angels." On the other hand, we see princes who pridefully refused to obey God, sometimes referred to as the "bad angels" or "fallen-away angels." How did this happen?

> In that period of probation one of the supreme Angels recognized his exceeding power, beauty and knowledge but failed to give thanks and glory to God. He became envious and intolerant of God's supreme dominion, and thereby he constituted himself as the adversary of God: he became Satan.[54]

The devil had perfect knowledge and complete freedom, yet chose a sinister path without influence from any other being, making his sin inexcusable. Because of his exalted position in the heavenly hosts, many angels followed Satan in his deranged crusade of hate and rebellion, likewise refusing obedience to God. Consequently, they were damned to hell for all eternity and desire nothing more than to pull all created beings down with them. They are sentenced to an existence of pain and torment. Thus, we see the consequences of using power in either the spirit of love and obedience or the spirit of hatred and defiance. The former leads to joy and salvation. The latter leads to destruction and damnation.

In light of the battle that raged in the heavens, the devoted Principalities stand out for mankind as a model of joyful obedience. They understood that God's authority is singular and primary, and following it is as necessary as the need for a human being to breathe. Made in the image and likeness of God, we are called to such obedience by the merits of our Baptism. Our baptismal promises compel us to completely submit our intellect and will to God and to constantly give our assent to Him with our whole being. Indeed, we not only follow Him, but belong entirely to Him. The *Catechism of the Catholic Church* refers to this as "the obedience of faith":

> To obey (from the Latin *ob-audire,* to "hear or to listen to") in faith is to submit freely to the word that has been heard, because its truth is guaranteed by God, who is Truth itself. Abraham is the model of such obedience offered us by Sacred Scripture. The Virgin Mary is the most perfect embodiment.[55]

Abraham (Abram) is known as the "father of all who believe" because of his exceptional faith and obedience to God. He was commanded to leave his home and family and set out to the Promised Land, not knowing exactly where it was, what the journey would cost him, or what he would face when he got there. He knew only that he must obey God and follow His directions, which he desired to do with all his heart. He persisted in his obedience to God, even when he believed he had been required to offer his beloved son, Isaac, as a holocaust (sacrifice).

Even more perfect in faith and obedience to God is the Blessed Virgin Mary. When the Archangel Gabriel appeared to her and asked her to do the seemingly impossible, she boldly proclaimed that nothing is impossible with God. She asked one question only: "How can this be, since I am a virgin?"[56] When the angel explained that the power of God would cause her to miraculously conceive His Son, she simply responded, "Here am I, the servant of the Lord; let it be with me according to your word."[57] Mary's faith and obedience never wavered throughout her life, even though she faced possible endangerment when granting God's request: She hastened to help her elderly cousin Elizabeth; when she fled to Egypt to protect Jesus' life; searched three days for Him when He had been lost; witnessed the threats against Him during His public ministry; and endured with Him the sufferings of His Passion and Crucifixion. Her superior obedience continued as He lay in the Tomb, rose on the third day, and left her to help guide the early Church after the Ascension. We might imagine that in each of these trials, she calmly murmured, "Nothing is impossible with God." We are called to do the same.

Examining the Influence of Wrath

The dictionary meaning of "wrath" is "vindictive anger, strong, stern, or fierce anger and deeply resentful indignation."[58] What better way to describe the attitude and actions of the fallen angels? Their pride and jealousy of God's beauty and supreme dominion certainly display vindictive anger and resentful indignation — wrath. Sadly, human beings also are prone to such deadly attitudes and actions. We allow resentment, pride, and jealousy to infiltrate our minds and hearts, eating away at them like leprosy and sentencing us to the bane of wrath. Wrath leads to hatred, and hatred separates us both from our fellow human beings and from God's grace. When we are separated from God's grace, we are in grave danger of losing our salvation.

Scripture is quite clear on the dangers of wrath in both the Old and New Testaments. The Psalmist warns:

Refrain from anger and forsake wrath.
Do not fret — it leads only to evil.
For the wicked shall be cut off,
> but those who wait for the LORD shall inherit
> the land.[59]

Saint Paul deeply loved the fledgling Christian communities he had founded. His sole endeavor was to reveal the truth to them, share with them the Good News, and lead them away from their former corrupt and sinful ways. He wrote to the Ephesians:

> Put away from you all bitterness and wrath and anger and wrangling and slander, together with all malice, and be kind to one another, tenderhearted, forgiving one another, as God in Christ has forgiven you.[60]

To the Colossians he wrote,

> Put to death, therefore, whatever in you is earthly: fornication, impurity, passion, evil desire, and greed (which is idolatry). On account of these the wrath of God is coming on those who are disobedient. These are the ways you also once followed, when you were living that life. But now you must get rid of all such things — anger, wrath, malice, slander, and abusive language from your mouth. Do not lie to one another, seeing that you have stripped off the old self with its practices and have clothed yourselves with the new self, which is being renewed in knowledge according to the image of its creator.[61]

In addition to decaying our minds and hearts, our wrath may draw God's wrath down upon us:

> For the wrath of God is revealed from heaven against all ungodliness and unrighteousness of men, who by their unrighteousness suppress the truth.[62]

In his Letter to the Romans, St. Paul sternly warned that God alone is permitted to exercise wrath, and we must never seek to avenge the wrongs (perceived or real) done to us.[63] We also must not let ourselves be provoked to wrath by day-to-day people or situations, prejudices or judgments that spark annoyance in us. Letting ill feelings stew in our hearts is a precursor to uncontrolled wrath. In his Letter to the Ephesians, St. Paul gives sound advice for acknowledging and dealing with our anger before it turns into sinful wrath. He wrote, "Be angry but do not sin; do not let the sun go down on your anger, and do not make room for the devil."[64] We can avoid this by practicing the advice in Proverbs:

> A soft answer turns away wrath, but a harsh word stirs up anger. The tongue of the wise dispenses knowledge, but the mouths of fools pour out folly.[65]

Let us then invoke the Principalities to intercede on our behalf for the grace and prudence to ardently obey God's commands and fiercely oppose the influence of wrath.

Facing Your Personal Challenges

Saint Peter was an impetuous and short-tempered person. You might think of him as a "holy hothead" who allowed his anger to get the best of him even to the point of violence.

We see this in the Garden of Gethsemane on the evening of Holy Thursday. Our Lord and His apostles had just finished the Passover meal (the Last Supper) together, and He had gone to the garden to pray. He took with Him Peter, James, and John. He had asked them to keep watch and pray with Him, but the apostles — tired after a good meal — fell asleep. As they slept, the soldiers entered the garden and asked which man was Jesus. After being betrayed by Judas Iscariot, Jesus identified Himself and freely allowed Himself to be bound in chains. He knew that the time had come for His Passion and Crucifixion and was ready to endure what was to come. But Peter, angered at the turn of events, would have none of it and was overcome with wrath:

> Suddenly, one of those with Jesus put his hand on his sword, drew it, and struck the slave of the high

priest, cutting off his ear. Then Jesus said to him, "Put your sword back into its place; for all who take the sword will perish by the sword. Do you think that I cannot appeal to my Father, and he will at once send me more than twelve legions of angels? But how then would the scriptures be fulfilled, which say it must happen in this way?"[66]

Peter deeply loved our Lord and had a right to feel angry. He did not, however, have the right to be moved to wrath and subsequently commit violence. Jesus' scolding of Peter was a sharp reminder that God alone is permitted to exercise wrath.

To a greater or lesser degree, there is a Peter inside each of us. We might feel anger — even righteous anger — and get so lost in our emotions that it soon turns to wrath. At those times we must remember Jesus' warning that those who live by the sword die by the sword. If we exert wrath upon another, God will exert His wrath upon us in the same measure.

Questions for Reflection

- Is there a "Peter" inside of me? How much so?
- Have I ever been overcome with wrath? What provoked it?
- Have I ever been the recipient of wrath? How did it affect me?
- What can I concretely do to avoid wrath, especially in provocative situations?

Resolutions

Practice deep breathing for 10 minutes twice daily. As you slowly inhale, envision the air entering your body as the Holy Spirit entering. As you slowly exhale, envision all the negative thoughts and emotions leaving your body. Surrender them to God, asking Him to lift them from you forever.

Invoking the Principalities

O Holy Principalities,

You exemplify perfect obedience. How painful it must have been to see members of your own choir defy God and refuse to obey him! You could have done the same and yet you remained faithful. Thank you for your faithfulness and for your willingness to help me be as obedient to God as you are. You are truly heavenly princes, deserving of my honor and love.

I ask you to be princes over my life, family, parish, community, and country. You symbolize God's princeliness and authoritativeness, and are guardians over governments, kingdoms, and nations as well as those who govern them. Please use your princely power to bring the world to peace and all nations back to God. Just as a military general commands and plans the operations of his troops, please command and plan for the Church on its pilgrimage toward Heaven. Help us to be victorious in our battle against Satan.

By the intercession of St. Michael and the celestial Choir of Principalities, may God fill our souls with a true spirit of obedience.

Amen.

DAY 8

Invoking the Choir of Archangels
Resist Despair

Learning from God's Messengers:
The Choir of Archangels

The Choir of Archangels is the most known and loved choir in popular devotion, the most famous of which are St. Michael, St. Gabriel, and St. Raphael. Saint Michael is referred to as the Prince of the Heavenly Host and the only one directly called thus in Scripture. Saint Gabriel is the messenger of the Incarnation, and St. Raphael is the angel of healing and of medicine.

Tradition holds that there are seven Archangels, but we know of only three because their names are specifically mentioned in Scripture. The names of the other four are not used in either Scripture or Liturgy, but some of the apocryphal books of the Bible (Enoch, for instance) assign names to them. These are used by some of the Eastern Orthodox Churches but are not found in the Western Church because they do not appear in the canonical books. Pope Zachary rejected them in 745 A.D., and they again were rejected in a synod held at Aix-la-Chappelle in 789 A.D.[67]

It seems that the seven Archangels have from the beginning been given a special place in God's plan and they are entrusted with extraordinary missions. Because of their high place, they are often called Archangel Princes in the writings of the saints, connoting their esteemed place of leadership and authority in the heavenly realm. Spiritual authors and mystics cite their special assistance, often attributing their protection or patronage to groups of seven (virtues, gifts of the Holy Spirit, etc.). During John's vision on the Island of Patmos, Christ instructed him to write down everything he saw and send it to the seven churches: Ephesus, Smyrna, Pergamum, Thyatira, Sardis, Philadelphia, and Laodicea.[68] Like the Principalities, the Archangels also are associated with the protection of nations, dioceses, religious communities, and the mission of the Church.

The three named Archangels — Michael, Gabriel, and Raphael — appear throughout both the Old and New Testaments.

The name Raphael comes from the Hebrew *rapha'*: to heal, and *'el*: God, meaning "God heals" or the "Divine Healer." The story of Tobit and Tobias contains the grandest appearance of an angel before a human, and it revolves around the manifestation of the Archangel Raphael, who disguised himself as a beautiful young man named Azarias. Raphael guided Tobias on his long and difficult journey to a foreign country. Tobias had no idea that the person he had hired was not a human, but rather an archangel. Only at the end of his long mission did Raphael reveal his true identity and name and the purpose of his mission:

> I will now declare the whole truth to you and will conceal nothing from you. Already I have declared it to you when I said, "It is good to conceal the secret of a king, but to reveal with due honor the works of God." So now when you and Sarah prayed, it was I who brought and read the record of your prayer before the glory of the Lord, and likewise whenever you would bury the dead. And that time when you did not hesitate to get up and leave your dinner to go and bury the dead, I was sent to you to test you. And at the same time God sent me to heal you and Sarah your daughter-in-law. I am Raphael, one of the seven angels who stand ready and enter before the glory of the Lord.[69]

Here Raphael reveals himself as a divine healer, not only of physical infirmities, such as the blindness of old Tobit, but also of spiritual afflictions and diabolical infestations, as in the case of Sarah, Tobias' wife. If he had not taken on a human form, it might not have been possible for Raphael to relate to men in such a familiar way and over such a long period of time. Had they known he was actually an archangel, they would have been fearful, and that would have subverted Raphael's angelic mission.

Was there anything immoral or deceptive about St. Raphael's behavior and assuming a human identity? Father Pascale Parente negates this assumption by pointing out that the archangel acted as proxy for Azarias, a young Israelite and relative of Tobias. During their time together, Raphael taught Tobias many important things and brought peace and happiness to two God-fearing but very unhappy families. He showed great medical knowledge and experience, and taught Tobias the same. He convinced Tobias to marry Sarah and freed her from the clutches of Satan. The instructions that Raphael gave to Tobias regarding marriage remain an ideal of moral perfection for married couples for all time. "We are the children of the saints, and we must not be joined together like heathens that know not God," Tobias explained to Sarah after his journey. Raphael perceptively sped up the journey home to save Tobit and his wife from further worry about the safety of their son during the arduous journey. Once the travelers had returned, Raphael cured Tobias of his blindness. After all had been accomplished, Raphael explained everything that had happened and why he had assumed the identity of Azarias. Then just as suddenly as he had appeared, Raphael returned to his invisible form and to the company of the other angels.[70]

Raphael's mission as healer did not stop there, however. During the time of our Lord, he was in Jerusalem at the pool of Bethsaida by the Sheep Gate. The pool was surrounded by five porticoes filled with a multitude of sick and disabled people who were waiting for the action of the angel upon the water of the pool. This action would immediately cure any person who was the first to enter the pool. "An Angel of the

Lord used to come down at certain times into the pool and the water was moved. And he that went down first into the pool after the motion of the water, was cured of whatever infirmity he had."[71]

We still can witness the healing ministry of the Archangel Raphael in the miraculous cures that have taken place even in our present times in many of the sacred shrines and holy places throughout the Christian world.

The name Gabriel means "God is my strength" or "the strength of God," and he has the special mission to communicate the Gospel, according to Mike Aquilina in his book *Angels of God: The Bible, the Church, and the Heavenly Hosts.*[72] We first encounter Gabriel by name in the Book of Daniel, where the prophet has a strange vision and Gabriel appears to explain it to him. The vision, he told Daniel, showed the future coming of the "Prince of princes," the Messiah. It was Gabriel who announced the birth of St. John the Baptist to Zechariah, and Gabriel who appeared to Mary to issue God's request for her to become the mother of Jesus. This demonstrated his exceptional wisdom, tact, and adroitness as he graciously handled her surprised reaction. He then had to allay her concerns over the protection of her virginity, answer her question ("How can this be, since I am a virgin?"), and prepare her for maternity. Finally, he reminded Mary that "nothing is impossible with God" by informing her that her elderly cousin, Elizabeth, was in her sixth month of pregnancy, despite being barren. Gabriel departed from Mary's side to bring the joyous news of the Incarnation to the other angels.

As St. Gabriel has the special role of messenger in God's plan of salvation, it seems plausible that he brought the "tidings of great joy" to the shepherds in their fields at the Nativity and could be the angel who warned Joseph in a dream to flee to Egypt to protect the life of the Child. It also is quite possible that it was Gabriel who told Joseph when it was safe to return to the land of Israel. We could wonder whether this special messenger of God was the angel who ministered to our Lord during His agony in the Garden of Gethsemane and the first to announce to the world the triumph of the Resurrection. Additionally, we could expect that it was he who rolled back the stone from Christ's tomb and told the women that He had risen:

> And suddenly there was a great earthquake; for an angel of the Lord, descending from heaven, came and rolled back the stone and sat on it. His appearance was like lightning, and his clothing white as snow. For fear of him the guards shook and became like dead men. But the angel said to the women, "Do not be afraid; I know that you are looking for Jesus who was crucified. He is not here; for he has been raised, as he said. Come, see the place where he lay. Then go quickly and tell his disciples, 'He has been raised from the dead, and indeed he is going ahead of you to Galilee; there you will see him.' This is my message for you."[73]

Furthermore, Gabriel's role as messenger suggests that he will be the angel to call the dead to life and to judgment at the end of time:

> For the Lord himself, with a cry of command, with the archangel's call and with the sound of God's trumpet, will descend from heaven, and the dead in Christ will rise first. Then we who are alive, who are left, will be caught up in the clouds together with them to meet the Lord in the air; and so, we will be with the Lord forever.[74]

Saint Michael's name comes from the Hebrew *Mikha'el*, meaning: *Who is like God?* His name itself is a battle cry — a shield and weapon in the struggle for eternal victory.[75] He is mentioned in the Book of Daniel when the angel who appeared to the prophet informed him that St. Michael would help him to defeat the evil princes of Persia and Greece. He is also mentioned in the Book of Jude when he contended with the devil and feuded over the body of Moses (see Jude 1:9). We find him more prominently however, in the Book of Revelation, where he fights in a dramatic battle against Satan and the other fallen angels:

And war broke out in heaven; Michael and his angels fought against the dragon. The dragon and his angels fought back, but they were defeated, and there was no longer any place for them in heaven. The great dragon was thrown down, that ancient serpent, who is called the Devil and Satan, the deceiver of the whole world — he was thrown down to the earth, and his angels were thrown down with him.[76]

Even though he belongs to a relatively low order by nature, St. Michael's outstanding zeal for the glory of God and the salvation of the other angels earns him the title "Prince of the Heavenly Host." This gives good reason to believe that he may be the very highest of all the angels because of the power granted him by God. He is God's legate who can speak and act in His name and by His authority. He has been and always will be the warrior angel who, from the beginning, has fought Satan and his demons, and throughout time, all the enemies of God's people, both human and diabolical.

We can learn much about the Archangels, especially St. Michael, from St. Faustina. She had great reverence for St. Michael; as mentioned earlier, as she wrote in her *Diary*, "He had no example to follow in doing the will of God, and yet he fulfilled God's will faithfully."[77]

We also know from her *Diary* that St. Faustina had an encounter with an angel that she described as "one of the seven spirits":

> Then I saw one of the seven spirits near me, radiant as at other times, under a form of light. I constantly saw him beside me when I was riding on the train. I saw an angel standing on every church we passed, but surrounded by a light that was paler than that of the spirit who was accompanying me on the journey, and each of these spirits who were guarding the churches bowed his head to the spirit who was near me.[78]

Since St. Faustina wrote of her regard for St. Michael and he is one of the seven spirits, or Archangels, mentioned in

Scripture, is it possible that it was St. Michael who accompanied her on the train?

An incident that occurred one night as St. Faustina was in her cell echoes the way Scripture has described St. Michael. That night, she saw an angel she referred to as "the executor of divine wrath." He was clothed in a dazzling robe, his face was gloriously bright, and he stood upon a cloud. Bolts of thunder and flashes of lightning were springing into his hands from the cloud and from his hands they went forth, striking the earth. Saint Faustina begged the angel to stop and give the world a chance to do penance. Then she saw the Holy Trinity and was pierced by Its majesty and greatness. From there, she was placed before the throne of God and pleaded with Him for the sake of mankind with the refrain of the Chaplet of Divine Mercy. Thus, the angel was rendered helpless in carrying out his punishment.[79]

Saint Faustina was again visited by one of the seven spirits during Adoration one day. As she adored our Lord in His Real Presence, she became overcome with love for Him. She was so overcome that she began to cry and suddenly saw "a spirit of great beauty." The spirit spoke to her and said, "Don't cry — says the Lord." When she asked the spirit who he was, he responded, "I am one of the seven spirits who stand before the throne of God day and night and give him ceaseless praise." This experience increased her longing for God. She later recalled, "This spirit is very beautiful and his beauty comes from close union with God. This spirit does not leave me for a single moment but accompanies me everywhere."[80]

Who Are the Archangels?

As mentioned in the previous chapter, there is substantial similarity between the Choir of Principalities and the Choir of Archangels. Saint Thomas Aquinas pointed this out in his *Summa Theologica*. While there are distinctions between the Principalities, Archangels, and Angels, there also is an overlap, or gradation, of characteristics and duties. This seems more pronounced between the Principalities and Archangels than between the Archangels and Angels. "A medium compared to one extreme seems like the other, as participating in the nature of both extremes; thus, tepid seems cold compared to hot, and hot compared to cold," he wrote. Just as the Principalities are considered princes of Heaven, so too do the Archangels receive princely esteem —both because of their office and because they preside over the Order of Angels and announce greater things.[81] Father O'Connell observed:

> The name does not, as it would seem, imply any authority over the angels of the inferior choir, but only a greater degree of dignity in the ministry which they exercise. For whereas the angels are deputed for the guardianship of private individuals, the Archangels have care of personages of exalted rank, such as kings, pontiffs and other rulers; and whereas angels are employed for the bestowal of personal favors on ordinary people, Archangels are the agents in the case of benefits affecting the public at large, and in all matters of graver moment.[82]

The Archangels are given the privilege and function of receiving, revealing, and displaying the highest celestial secrets to humanity. Their name comes from the Greek *archos*, which means the first, and *angelus*, messenger. They have the highest and purest intentions, and prophecy for God to humanity.[83]

Our Lord often speaks of "Gehenna" and of "the unquenchable fire" that is reserved for those who refuse to be converted even to the end of their lives. In such cases, both soul and body can be lost.[84] Jesus has proclaimed that He "will send his angels, and they will collect out of his kingdom all causes of sin and all evil doers, and they will throw them into the furnace of fire, where there will be weeping and gnashing of teeth. He will pronounce the condemnation: 'You that are accursed, depart from me into the eternal fire prepared for the devil and his angels.'"[85]

The angels of whom Jesus spoke are the Archangels who will carry out His justice in the final hour. God in His wisdom and mercy has given us these divine creatures as guides and protectors in the battle against Satan, his demons, and their influence in our lives.

The Eighth Salutation:
For the Grace to Persevere in Faith and All Good Works

When I did a speaking engagement in Ireland a few years ago, I had the privilege of tracing the path of St. Patrick and visiting Croagh Patrick (Patrick's Stack) in County Mayo. Croagh Patrick, or "The Reek" as it is locally known, is the Holy Mountain for the Irish people. It was a pagan site of worship dating back to 3000 B.C., on which rituals in appeasement of the pagan deities were performed — including human sacrifice. In 441 A.D., St. Patrick spent the 40 days of Lent praying and fasting on the mountaintop as penance and petition for the conversion of Ireland to the Catholic faith.

At more than 2,500 feet high, Croagh Patrick is both majestic and arduous to climb. Its ominously steep slopes are a reminder of the grave dangers and persecutions St. Patrick endured to Christianize the Emerald Isle. It is a monument and tribute to his heroic perseverance of faith.

Saint Patrick is referred to as the apostle of Ireland. It is supposed that he was born around 389 A.D. In about 406 A.D., he, along with many others, was carried off from his home in England by raiders who sold him into slavery to the pagan inhabitants of Ireland. Rather than corrupt him, his hardships made him grow in holiness.

After six years, he had a vision that he would soon be freed, and shortly thereafter he escaped captivity and ended up in Gaul. At the age of 23, he was able to make his way back to his homeland. He was happy for a time, but then began to receive visions of the people of Ireland pleading with him to return. "We beseech thee, holy youth, to come and walk among us once more," the voices said.

It is not certain exactly how or when Patrick did indeed return, gather around him many disciples, and enthusiastically embark on the work of evangelizing Ireland. Although he had many faithful disciples, many others scorned him. He was installed as archbishop of Armagh to replace the previous bishop, who had been murdered. He was unjustly imprisoned, constantly threatened by the pagans who preferred him dead,

and faced opposition and scrutiny from the Church, which
was skeptical of his methods of catechizing.

Despite these trials, he managed to maintain communi-
cation with his contacts abroad, including Pope St. Leo the
Great. In 444 A.D., the See of Ireland was founded along
with the Cathedral Church of Armagh, an administration and
education center.

There are no accurate records, but it is possible that St.
Patrick died and was buried in or around 461 A.D. at Saul on
Strangford Lough, where he had built his first church.[86]

The tireless fervor of St. Patrick in living both his faith
and his mission can only be gained through an ardent life of
prayer rooted in love, and we also must strive for this. The
Catechism tells us that in order "to live, grow, and persevere
in the faith until the end we must nourish it with the word
of God; we must beg the Lord to increase our faith, and it
must be 'working through charity,' abounding in hope, and
rooted in the faith of the Church."[87] We must long for the
grace of final perseverance and the reward of Heaven based on
our good works.

For me, and I would think many others, St. Patrick is a
solid example of bold perseverance in faith. Did he have extra
help from the Archangels to carry out his mission? Most probably, especially since his mission included directing the fate of
an entire country.

In *The Breastplate of St. Patrick* prayer, he invokes the
angels for protection and pledges himself to their service:

I arise today
Through a mighty strength, the invocation of the Trinity,
Through belief in the Threeness,
Through confession of the Oneness
    of the Creator of creation.

I arise today
Through the strength of Christ's birth with His baptism,
Through the strength of His crucifixion with His burial,
Through the strength of His resurrection with
    His ascension,

Through the strength of His descent for the judgment
of doom.

I arise today
Through the strength of the love of Cherubim,
In the obedience of angels,
In the service of Archangels,
In the hope of resurrection to meet with reward.[88]

Like St. Patrick, we must invoke the Archangels for perseverance and faith in all good works so that we may live joyfully in
eternity with God.

Examining the Influence of Despair

Despair is the complete loss of hope, especially hope in God's
mercy and kindness. Satan wants nothing more than to draw us
into despair because then we will lose sight of God, so to speak,
and deny His abundant grace. We see this particularly in people
who have strayed from the faith and no longer have attachment
to God. The image of God is then disfigured in them:

> Very often, deceived by the Evil One, men have
> become vain in their reasonings, and have exchanged
> the truth of God for a lie, and served the creature
> rather than the Creator. Or else, living and dying in
> this world without God, they are exposed to ulti-
> mate despair.[89]

The *Catechism* reminds us:

> The first commandment is also concerned with sins
> against hope, namely, despair and presumption: by
> despair, man ceases to hope for his personal salvation
> from God, for help in attaining it for the forgiveness
> of his sins. Despair is contrary to God's goodness, to
> his justice — for the Lord is faithful to his promises
> — and to his mercy.[90]

Multiple situations can tempt us to despair. It is not uncom-
mon to see someone who has suffered a broken relationship or

loss of self-worth, is trapped in a difficult living environment, or harbors deep regrets that give way to despair. At the root of some addictions (such as to drugs or alcohol) is despair, because people fail to find their hope and consolation in God. Despair surfaces when we are caught in a situation with seemingly no resolution or remedy. We even can approach despair when we think that God is not hearing or answering our prayers.

Illness and suffering are among the gravest problems we confront. When we are ill, we experience our own powerlessness and limitations. Each illness gives us a glimpse of death:

> Illness can lead to anguish, self-absorption, sometimes even despair and revolt against God. It can also make a person more mature, helping him discern in his life what is not essential so that he can turn toward that which is. Very often illness provokes a search for God and a return to him.[91]

Those who despair are distanced from God and in danger of losing the promise of eternity. Despair blocks us from God's grace and closes our hearts to a loving and lasting relationship with him.

Facing Your Personal Challenges

With all the hardships, suffering, and opposition St. Patrick faced, he had good cause for despair. At times, it must have seemed like all was lost or that it was just too risky to continue his work. Yet he never wavered in his resolve.

There was a time in my life when it seemed as though all was lost. It was not due to opposition, but rather from a physical ailment. I had an extremely painful spine condition that was not responding to non-invasive treatments. Eventually it became so painful and debilitating that I could no longer stand it, and I opted for major spine surgery. I did my research and thought I was fully prepared for what was to come. I knew it would not be easy, but I had no idea how truly hard it would be.

The surgery itself was a spectacular success; however, the incision did not heal properly and had to be reopened to force the healing process to begin all over again. The wound beneath the surface was several inches long and quite deep — right down to the spine in some spots.

Try as the doctors might, the wound did not want to close on its own, and so I was referred to a wound specialist who scraped the wound and put me on a negative pressure wound therapy machine (wound VAC, for short) that I had to be attached to 24/7. The machine hung from a shoulder strap, tubing ran from the machine to my back, and it was *noisy*. As you can imagine, sleeping and carrying on normal everyday life became a challenge, and being in public was embarrassing.

This went on for more than six months with at first biweekly and then weekly visits to the doctor's office. I was already deeply disappointed that I had to wear the wound VAC; as time went on I was drawing closer and closer to true despair. I felt abandoned by God and found it difficult to pray with a sincere heart.

Thanks be to God, the wound finally did heal completely and my spine is fully functional. I feel better, stronger, and more agile than I have in more than a decade.

I consider myself a faithful servant of God and ardent prayer warrior. Yet I shudder to look back and realize how close I had been to succumbing to despair.

Questions for Reflection

- What impresses me about the story of St. Patrick?
- What do I admire about the Archangels?
  Which one do I most admire?
- What does my relationship with the Archangels look like, and how can I deepen it?
- Have I ever been moved to despair?
  When and why?

Resolutions

Sit quietly for a short time, breathing deeply and placing yourself in the presence of the Holy Spirit. Go back to a time when you were genuinely tempted to despair. Think about what led you there and what led you out of it. Consider how you might approach such situations differently in the future.

Invoking the Archangels

O Holy Archangels,

You have been given a special place in God's plan and have been entrusted with extraordinary missions. Your importance is not lessened by the fact that there are seven of you. Perhaps instead this increases your importance. I know only three of you by name, and yet I love and honor you all.

Saint Michael, you are the Prince of the Heavenly Host and a valiant leader in the battle against

Satan. Help me, please, to be valiant against Satan throughout my life. Defend me from his treachery.

Saint Gabriel, you brought God's message to human beings in some of the most monumental moments in human history, above all, the Incarnation. Let me never forget the importance of your messages and the impact they hold on my life and salvation.

Saint Raphael, you are the angel of healing and medicine. I am afflicted both physically and spiritually. Please use your healing powers on my behalf.

By the intercession of St. Michael and the celestial Choir of Archangels, may the Lord give us perseverance in faith and in all good works, in order that we gain the glory of Paradise.

Amen.

DAY 9

Invoking the Choir of Angels
Resist Fear

Learning from God's Messengers:
The Choir of Angels

The Choir of Angels are the last and lowest choir in the hierarchy of angels, but by no means the least important. When compared with the higher orders, the Angels are the least perfect although in comparison to our human nature they are superiorly perfect. According to St. Thomas Aquinas, the higher choirs have a more universal knowledge than the lower ones and can know things more perfectly that the lower choirs.[92] It is in some ways unfortunate that we so commonly use the term "angels" to refer to all the angelic spirits since this diminishes the attention and honor this final choir deserves.

By their nature and duties, the Angels are closer to man than any of the other choirs and are the closest link between the spirit world and rational man. They are most involved in the doings of mankind and are those sent out on missions from God and from whom the Guardian Angels are chosen. They are ordinarily — but not exclusively — taken for the guidance and protection of individual souls while on earth.[93]

The Angels in the Choir of Angels are, in some ways, the most beloved and best known by humans among the choirs because God has placed them at our sides to watch over and care for us on a very personal level. They are the ministers of Christ's love and are our faithful protectors, defending us against harm and temptation. So, too, they warn us of impending evil and encourage us to remain faithful to God in prayer.

Usually, they are the only choir who specifically accomplishes works involving individual persons.[94]

The Angels are not only our guardians and protectors, but also our companions. Should we allow it, our relationship with them would be one of deep and abiding friendship. It is almost as if we could hang out with them as we do with our human friends and family. These beautiful and powerful creatures were sent entirely for our benefit and take their responsibilities and relationship with us quite seriously. The most remarkable thing about our relationship with the Angels is that they are fully present to us and fully present to God at the same time. This is possible only because they are powerful and intelligent spirits completely devoted to God.

After the Transfiguration, Jesus and His disciples traveled to Capernaum, teaching and healing along the way. He knew that the time for His Passion and Crucifixion was rapidly nearing, and He had much to teach them. Kibitzing among themselves, the disciples wanted to know who is greatest in Heaven. Unable to resolve this among themselves, they posed the question to our Lord. He answered them by calling a child to Himself and standing the child before them. He warned them that the only way to enter the Kingdom of Heaven is to become innocent, trusting, humble, and loving like the child. Additionally, He taught that anyone who welcomes such a child welcomes Christ Himself. He then went on to address the dangers of temptation to sin and again referred to the child. He pointed out the contrast between the untainted child and the besmirched adult. His words have great bearing on our understanding of the Angels and their role in our lives. His words are worth praying over:

> If any of you put a stumbling block before one of these little ones who believe in me, it would be better for you if a great millstone were fastened around your neck and you were drowned in the depth of the sea. Woe to the world because of stumbling blocks! Occasions for stumbling are bound to come, but woe to the one by whom the stumbling block comes![95]

Take care that you do not despise one of these little ones; for, I tell you, in heaven their angels continually see the face of my Father in heaven. What do you think? If a shepherd has a hundred sheep, and one of them has gone astray, does he not leave the ninety-nine on the mountains and go in search of the one that went astray? And if he finds it, truly I tell you, he rejoices over it more than over the ninety-nine that never went astray. So it is not the will of your Father in heaven that one of these little ones should be lost.[96]

In the first passage, we are reminded of God's affection for even the simplest of souls and passion for protecting them. We, too, are children of God and must become childlike to gain Heaven. In the second passage, we are reminded that each child of God is unique and precious, and therefore we must never tempt one another. He placed special emphasis on the grave offense of leading children away from God or failing to foster in them a true love for Him. Those who subvert the godliness of the next generation will suffer deadly consequences. Finally, Jesus assures us of the love, vigilance, and protection of our Angels.

Who Are the Angels?

For he will command his angels concerning you
　to guard you in all your ways.
On their hands they will bear you up,
　so that you will not dash your foot against a stone.
You will tread on the lion and the adder,
　the young lion and the serpent you will trample
under foot.[97]

This verse from the Psalms charmingly describes the Angels' activity in our lives. At God's command, they watch over us in everything we think, do, and speak. They are constantly with us, never tiring nor becoming distracted from their duties. Their capabilities and devotion are far beyond that of any human being, even the persons whom we most ardently trust and by whom we are cherished. There is not a single moment in which Guardian Angels do not know where we are, how we are, and what we are doing. They even are aware of what we are thinking and feeling. They are sensitive to our needs, emotions, and vulnerabilities. They are cognizant of impending danger long before we are and will divert us from harm, even something as simple as tripping over a rock while on a hike! Father Horgan observes:

> In their ministry, the Angels are conscientious and faithful. When they stand by our side, God sees us joined to them. And so, we can hardly do better than to ask the Lord to help us to draw closer and closer into the fidelity that characterizes the life of the Angels.[98]

If we trust our Angels to care for and protect us, they will not fail in their commission. God has willed it to be so.

We can safely assume that there are vast numbers of Angels. Our Lord Himself said so when He told Peter in the Garden of Gethsemane at the time of His arrest, "Do you think that I cannot appeal to my Father, and he will at once send me more than twelve legions of angels?"[99] In Jesus' time, a legion of Roman soldiers consisted of nearly 7,000 men, and this metaphoric example uses the familiar to explain the unfamiliar. It appears that our Lord is impressing upon Peter — and us — that there are multitudes of Angels, all at His command.[100]

It is hard for us to imagine the myriad of angels created by God. Scripture does not give us an exact number, and yet it indicates that it must be a very large number. Is it more than the number of people in the entire United States? Is it more than the number of people in the entire world? We can only imagine. Realizing this, what an amazing sight it would be to see the Psalmist's words come to pass:

> Praise the LORD!
> Praise the LORD from the heavens;
>   praise him in the heights!

Praise him, all his angels;
praise him, all his host![101]

Again at the Nativity, we glimpse the magnitude of the Angels when they appeared to the shepherds in the fields:

And suddenly there was with the angel a multitude of the heavenly host, praising God and saying,

Glory to God in the highest heaven, and on earth peace among those whom he favors![102]

In His goodness, the Heavenly Father has given us boun-teous mentors for our relationships with the Angels. We see in many of the saints outstanding devotion, not only to their Angels, but to the imitation of them in their lives.

One such saint is St. Hildegard of Bingen (1098–1179), who is an extraordinary example of monastic-angelic life. She understood her vocation to be an imitation of the Angels' life of praise and glorification of God. She expressed this in her writings, the illustrations of her manuscripts, and especially her music. She is an outstanding case of a woman who used all her talents, skills, and creativity to make her unique mental and mystical enlightenments available to others to bless them. She strove to make truths accessible to the human senses, often doing so with the miniatures she created depicting her mystical visions of Christ and His Angels.

Despite the many controversies that plagued her during her life, her mission in the life of the Church received recogni-tion and new impetus when Pope Benedict XVI declared her a Doctor of the Church in 2012.[103]

Another holy soul with a special relationship with the Angels was Blessed Anna Maria Taigi (1769–1837). She did everything consciously in the presence of her Guardian Angel, even sending him to comfort the sick and offer protection to those who are tempted to sin. The Angels repeatedly visited Blessed Anna Maria, a poor Roman housewife and mother of seven children, who was graced by God with phenomenal gifts of prophecy and prayer. She was illiterate, yet she could see events of the past, present, and future for the purpose of

bringing comfort and strength to Christ's Church, then bur-
dened with heavy crosses. She did this only through the grace
of God and the help of her Guardian Angel.[104]

Another such saint was St. Crescentia Hoess (1682–
1744), a German Franciscan mystic who also possessed the
mystical graces of great intimacy with her Guardian Angel, as
well as the Angels of souls in Purgatory who were the object
of her prayers, penances, and charity. The Angels also advised
her in her dealings with the other sisters and in giving them
encouragement to live a deeper spiritual life. She suffered
chronic poor health, including migraines and toothaches.
Later in life, arthritis crippled her hands and feet, causing her
to have a permanently crouched posture. All the while, her
Guardian Angel ministered to and strengthened her.[105]

Another saint who loved the holy Angels was St. Pio of
Pietrelcina (Padre Pio), the holy Franciscan mystic who died
in 1968 and bore the stigmata for more than 50 years. He
had such an intimate relationship with his Guardian Angel and
close contacts with other angels that several books have been
written about their friendship. Padre Pio called his angel the
"shining man" and saw him as a true and inseparable friend.
His Guardian Angel not only protected and guided him but at
times even preached to him. In his early letters, he stated that
his angel would correct him when he was not behaving as he
should. It was his angel who helped him adapt himself to his
mission to carry the Cross of Jesus in a visible and unending
Way of the Cross. He did this for more than 50 years under the
scrutiny of both friends and enemies, and it was his angel who
gave him the strength to do so.[106]

Then of course St. Faustina had a very close relationship
with her Guardian Angel, and wrote about him in her *Diary*
several times. He came to her rescue many times, revealed
Purgatory to her, and taught her to pray for the dying.

One time, her Guardian Angel approached her in the
garden and told her to pray for the dying. Immediately, St.
Faustina and the gardeners did as the angel said.[107] On another
occasion, her Guardian Angel alerted her to the needs of a
dying soul:

My Guardian Angel told me to pray for a certain soul, and in the morning I learned that it was a man whose agony had begun at that very moment. The Lord Jesus makes it known to me in a special way when someone is in need of prayer. ... I feel vividly and clearly that spirit who is asking me for prayer. I was not aware that souls are so closely united, and often it is my Guardian Angel who tells me.[108]

Saint Faustina's Guardian Angel also rescued her when she was threatened by the devil and needed protection. While asleep one night, she felt Satan shake her bed, instantly waking her. Instead of falling into fear, she began to pray to her Guardian Angel and was saved from the demon's antics.[109]

At another time, St. Faustina's Guardian Angel appeared to her in radiance and "a flame of fire sparkled from his forehead." Yet again, she was being blocked by a multitude of hatred-filled demons and prayed to her Guardian Angel for help. He appeared to her and said, "Do not fear, spouse of my Lord, without His permission these spirits will do you no harm." The evil spirits immediately vanished.[110]

From these saints and many others, we learn the value of the Angels, particularly our Guardian Angels, and the importance of diligently striving to imitate them. They are our personal gifts from God the Father, and thus we should yearn for a dear and lasting relationship with them.

The Ninth Salutation:
For Protection in This Life and Escort into Heaven

Our Angels are charged with our welfare and protection, and they accompany us from the moment of our conception until the moment of our death. It makes perfect sense that they would escort us into Heaven when our time has come.

We have proof of this in Jesus' parable of the Rich Man and Lazarus. The rich man was extravagantly dressed and feasted on sumptuous food every day. He seemingly had not a care in the world. A poor man named Lazarus lay at his gate. Lazarus was covered with sores and was starving. He longed to eat the scraps that fell from the rich man's table because even this would be better than what he had. He was in such a pathetic state that the dogs came and licked his sores. This man was humble and unassuming in every regard. When his body was no longer able to endure his pain, he died. "The poor man died and was carried away by the angels to be with Abraham," Jesus said (Lk 16:22). This is a clear indication that those who die in the grace of God are escorted into eternal life by their Angels.

There is no guarantee that we will automatically merit the reward of Heaven when we die. Therefore we must do our best to live a life of ardent devotion to God and compliance with His will and commands. We must sincerely repent of our sins, hope in salvation, trust in God's mercy, and consistently live our lives in the state of grace.

The *Catechism* has much to say about hope in the promise of Heaven:

> We can therefore hope in the glory of heaven promised by God to those who love him and do his will. In every circumstance, each one of us should hope, with the grace of God, to persevere to the end and to obtain the joy of heaven, as God's eternal reward for the good works accomplished with the grace of Christ. In hope, the Church prays for all men to be saved. She longs to be united with Christ, her Bridegroom, in the glory of heaven.[111]

It goes on to quote the great mystic, St. Teresa of Ávila:

> Hope, O my soul, hope. You know neither the day nor the hour. Watch carefully, for everything passes quickly, even though your impatience makes it doubtful what is certain, and it turns a very short time into a long one. Dream that the more you struggle, the more you prove the love that you bear your God, and the more you will rejoice one day with your Beloved, in a happiness and rapture that can never end.[112]

The Angels, particularly our Guardian Angels, give us reason for the hope of which St. Teresa of Ávila speaks. The desire for Heaven must be the guiding light of our lives with our Guardian Angels being reflections of that light. They guide us because of their profound desire for our salvation, and so we follow their promptings and relish their presence.

Examining the Influence of Fear

Fear is one of the principal passions, along with love, hatred, desire, joy, sadness, and anger. These passions are natural components of the human psyche as they form a connection between the life of the senses and the life of the mind. Jesus told us that the passions spring from the heart.

The most fundamental passion is love. Love causes us to desire an actual or perceived good and live in the hope of obtaining it. We feel fulfilled when we have obtained the desired good.[113] We might passionately love our spouse, fiancé, parents, siblings, or children. In these cases, of course, passionate love is meant in a virtuous sense. We might love our country in a patriotic sense, and we might love God's commandments in unison with our love for him.

Fear thwarts love and arises when the good is somehow threatened. This could be our possessions, home, financial security, physical safety, mental health, or position. We fear impending evil and harm. In some cases, fear is beneficial as when we are in a dangerous situation and must defend ourselves or loved ones. However, this fear must never take over our complete trust in God and protection of His Angels.

There is a form of fear that we must always feel, and that is the fear of God. It is one of the Seven Gifts of the Holy Spirit, along with wisdom, understanding, counsel, fortitude, knowledge, and piety. This kind of fear is a chaste and holy fear in reverence and respect for God and the avoidance of separating ourselves from Him. We love and trust in Him as Father, Son, and Holy Spirit, yet we fear His might, power, and justice.

Saint John Henry Newman spoke about healthy fear of God in one of his sermons:

Are these feelings of fear and awe Christian feelings or not? ... I say this, then, which I think no one can reasonably dispute. They are the class of feelings we *should* have — yes, have to an intense degree — if we literally had the sight of Almighty God; therefore they are the class of feelings which we shall have, *if* we realize His presence. In proportion as we believe that He is present, we shall have them; and not to have them, is not to realize, not to believe that He is present.[114]

When we forget that our valiant angel protectors are constantly beside us, we easily fall into a detrimental fear that causes nothing but misery. They are sent to us by God and are reflections of His omnipotence and strength. They are in essence "partnering" with God for our protection and salvation. They also can teach us how to foster a holy and life-giving fear of God that will draw us more deeply into His ever-loving presence.

Facing Your Personal Challenges

One of my favorite consoling Scripture passages comes from the Gospel of Matthew. Jesus had summoned His Apostles and was conferring on them the authority of the Church for the casting out of unclean spirits, disease, and illness. Once He had prepared them, He sent them out to find the lost sheep of Israel and proclaim the Good News. He instructed them to cure the sick, raise the dead, cleanse the lepers, cast out demons, and do so without payment. They were to take no possessions whatsoever with them and to depend entirely on Divine Providence.

He warned them that there were places they would not be welcome and homes they would have to leave because of hostility. He prophesied coming persecutions, telling them that He was sending them out like sheep into the midst of wolves and that they must be as wise as serpents and innocent as doves. He warned them that they would be hated for their Christian faith, handed over to counsels, flogged in the synagogues, and dragged before governors and kings. He promised them, however, that how they should act and what they should say at the time would be given to them by the Holy Spirit. He guaranteed that they would never be truly harmed if they clung to Him. It could be assumed that He also planned to employ His Angels for their protection:

> So have no fear of them; for nothing is covered up that will not be uncovered, and nothing secret that will not become known. What I say to you in the dark, tell in the light; and what you hear whispered, proclaim from the housetops. Do not fear those who kill the body but cannot kill the soul; rather fear him who can destroy both soul and body in hell. Are not two sparrows sold for a penny? Yet not one of them will fall to the ground apart from your Father. And even the hairs of your head are all counted. So do not be afraid; you are of more value than many sparrows.[115]

This passage, albeit a bit long, has been my go-to passage for courage and consolation in many threatening situations. It reminds me that no amount of pain, harm, travail, or persecution can cause me any real harm. The sufferings of this life are brief when compared to the glory of eternity. Once we are united with our Lord, these times of distress will be nothing more than a blink of the eye.

I am God's child and have the full protection of His Angels. Therefore, I need have no fear. "Do not fear those who kill the body but cannot kill the soul."[116]

Questions for Reflection

- What kind of relationship do I have with my Guardian Angel?
- How can I improve that relationship?
- Of what (who) am I most afraid?
- Why do I fear it (them)?

Resolutions

Review your answers to the Questions for Reflection. In your mind, place yourself back in a situation in which you were truly fearful. (Do not do this alone if you have suffered traumatic events. Do so only with the guidance of your spiritual director or trained professional.) Remember how you acted in that situation. Then imagine the situation again, but this time picture yourself with your Guardian Angel by your side and the other Angels surrounding you. Imagine yourself acting with courage and trust in God's protection rather than fear. How is the second scene different from the first?

Invoking the Angels

O Holy Angels,

There are vast numbers of you, and yet each one has an irreplaceable role in the plan of salvation. Of all the choirs in the celestial hierarchy, you have the closest relationship to human beings. You are not only guardians and protectors, but also companions. You have been sent entirely for my benefit and take your responsibilities and relationship with me quite seriously. You are present to God and to me at the same time. This is almost unimaginable to my primitive human mind.

You've been charged with my welfare and protection, and have been accompanying me since the moment I was conceived in my mother's womb. Since then, you have never left my side and you will never leave my side in the future. You will watch over and guard me throughout my life and, I pray, escort me into Heaven when the time comes.

My dear Angels, I yearn to have a deep and abiding relationship with you. Please help me to do that.

By the intercession of St. Michael and the celestial Choir of Angels, may the Lord grant us to be protected by them in this mortal life and conducted hereafter to eternal glory.

Amen.

Conclusion

As I worked to put the final touches on this manuscript, news broke of a popular music artist whose performance at the Grammy Awards was a pageant of demons dancing in hell with Baphomet as their leader. The central figure, flailing "dancers," and overall red glow was eerie and frightening. The fact that this happened at all is alarming. The fact that it happened in a worldwide and highly watched arena is appalling and literally dis-grace-ful. I watched only a few seconds of the fiasco (I could take no more), but it was long enough to catch not only the deadliness of the performance but the gleeful excitement of the audience.

After the performance, praise splattered the internet and airways, suggesting that this performer is a hero for his artistic boldness. This deeply grieves me. What grieves me even more is that this is just one example of such devilishness and devolution of morals; there are endless more.

This experience confirmed for me the absolute necessity and perfect timing of this book. Now more than ever we need St. Michael and his armies of angels to protect us from the evil one, who is pervading our world, our culture, and our lives. We must cling to Christ and to His angels for courage and protection. We must look to them for inspiration in our daily lives and striving for holiness. We must lean on them when we are surrounded by evil influences. Without them, we cannot stand strong against Satan and his treachery.

The Chaplet of St. Michael is an effective weapon in this battle. Saint Michael promised to whomever would pray this Chaplet:

- That he would send a chosen angel from each angelic choir to accompany the devotees at the time of Communion. To those who recite these nine salutations, every day:

- They will enjoy his continued assistance during this life and after death, in Purgatory, and

- They will be accompanied by all the angels and will be, with all their loved ones and relatives, freed from Purgatory.[117]

This book merely touches upon all the amazing attributes, personalities, and characteristics of the Choirs of Angels. It would take volumes to adequately address all of them!

I pray that this book will inspire in you an ardent devotion to the Prince of the Heavenly Host and inspire you to explore the angels and your relationship with them more fully. May you never forget that they are an encompassing and vital part of your life in this world and the next.

Saint Bernard of Clairvaux offered a beautiful description of the Choirs of Angels. I want to leave you with this last inspiration:

God loves in the Seraphim as charity, knows in the Cherubim as truth, is seated in the Thrones as equity, reigns in the Dominations as majesty, rules in the Principalities as principal, guards in the Powers as salvation, acts in the Virtues as strength, reveals in the Archangels as light, assists in the angels as piety.[118]

About the Author

 **Marge Steinhage Fenelon** is an award-winning journalist and author, internationally known speaker, life coach, retreat leader, and Catholic media personality. She has been published in dozens of Catholic and secular publications and is the author of several books about Marian devotion and Catholic spirituality and family life. Her book, *Our Lady, Undoer of Knots: A Living Novena,* received a 2016 Association of Catholic Publishers Award for Excellence in Publishing. *My Queen, My Mother: A Living Novena (A Marian Pilgrimage across America)* was awarded a Catholic Press Association Book Award, and *America's Mary: The Story of Our Lady of Good Help* has won wide acclaim and chronicles for the first time America's *only* Church-approved Marian apparition.

Marge has a bachelor's degree in public relations / journalism and worked for a time as a public relations consultant. She has a certificate in Marian studies from the International Marian Research Institute and a certificate in spiritual mentoring from Cardinal Stritch University.

In 2015, Marge was awarded the Egan Fellowship for Excellence in Journalism, traveling to the Philippines to report on the ongoing reconstruction efforts in the aftermath of Super Typhoon Hayan. Later that year, she was accepted to the Jordan Tourism Board Religious Journalist and Blogger Tour, exploring the many holy sites in the "other" Holy Land. She is an instructor for the Archdiocese of Milwaukee Permanent Deacon Wives Program.

For more about Marge, visit margefenelon.com.

Endnotes

[1] *Catechism of the Catholic Church*, 2nd ed. (Libreria Editrice Vaticana, 1994), sec. 1706. Hereafter *Catechism*.

[2] Peter Kreeft, *Angels (and Demons): What Do We Really Know about Them?* (Ignatius Press, 1995), 50.

[3] Ibid., 67.

[4] Ibid., 71–72.

[5] James F. Day, OP, *St. Michael the Archangel* (Our Sunday Visitor, 2020), 31–32.

[6] Sister Maria Faustina Kowalska, *Diary of Saint Maria Faustina Kowalska: Divine Mercy in My Soul* (Marian Press, 1987), 667. Hereafter *Diary*.

[7] *Diary*, 706.

[8] EWTN.com, "The Chaplet of St. Michael the Archangel," accessed June 23, 2023, www.ewtn.com/catholicism/devotions/Chaplet-of-st-michael-the-archangel-386.

[9] DiscerningHearts.com, "Chaplet of St. Michael the Archangel," accessed August 16, 2023, www.discerninghearts.com/catholic-podcasts/prayersdevotionals/Chaplet-of-st-michael-the-archangel. Used with permission.

[10] *Diary*, 676.

[11] *Catechism*, sec. 1822.

[12] *Diary*, 1717.

[13] *Encyclopedia Britannica Online*, s.v. "Ezekiel; Hebrew Prophet," accessed May 4, 2022, www.britannica.com/biography/Ezekiel-Hebrew-prophet.

[14] Henri-Marie Boudon, trans. Edward Healy Thompson, *Devotion to the Nine Choirs of Angels: Especially to Angel-Guardians* (Benziger Brothers, 1918), 151–152.

[15] Heb 9:4.

[16] *Bible Study Tools*, "Palm tree," accessed April 11, 2022, www.biblestudytools.com/dictionary/palm-tree.

[17] *Catechism*, sec. 2384.

[18] Ibid., sec. 2733.

[19] It could be argued that rulers and powers refer to human authorities or angelic ones.

[20] Saint Thomas Aquinas, *Summa Theologica*, trans. Fathers of the English Dominican Province (Coyote Canyon Press, 2010), I, Q 108, Art. 5, Obj. 6.

[21] John Horgan, *His Angels at Our Side: Understanding Their Power in Our Souls and the World* (EWTN Publishing, 2018), 24.

[22] Rev. Raphael V. O'Connell, SJ, *The Holy Angels* (P. J. Kenedy & Sons, 1923), 92.

[23] *Catechism*, sec. 2303.

[24] *Summa Theologica*, 900.

[25] Ibid., 89.

[26] *Catechism*, sec. 306.

[27] Horgan, *His Angels at Our Side*, 25.

[28] *Summa Theologica*, Obj. 2.

[29] Horgan, *His Angels at Our Side*, 89.

[30] *Catechism*, sec. 1763.

[31] Ibid., sec. 1764.

[32] Ibid., sec. 1772.

[33] Sandra Mardenfeld, "Does Sex Still Sell? What Marketers Should Know," BusinessNewsDaily.com, updated October 23, 2023, www.businessnewsdaily.com/2649-sex-sells-more.html.

[34] *Catechism*, sec. 2332.

[35] Alban Butler, *Butler's Lives of the Saints,* ed. Paul Burns (Liturgical Press, 2003), 207.

[36] *Summa Theologica*, 971.

[37] Ibid., 975.

[38] O'Connell, *Holy Angels*, 00.

[39] *Summa Theologica*, Art. 6, Obj. 4.

[40] O'Connell, *Holy Angels*, 87-88.

[41] Saint John Vianney, *The Little Catechism of The Cure of Ars: Selected Passage from the Writings of The Cure of Ars* (Tan Books, 1951), 84–85.

[42] *Summa Theologica*, 976.

[43] O'Connell, *Holy Angels*, 85–86.

[44] *Catechism*, sec. 407–409.

[45] *Gaudium et Spes,* Pastoral Constitution on the Church in the Modern World, December 7, 1965, 37 §2, www.vatican.va/archive/hist_councils/ii_vatican_council/documents/vat-ii_const_19651207_gaudium-et-spes_en.html.

[46] Rom 7:19–20.

[47] *Gaudium et Spes,* 13 §2.

[48] *Catechism*, sec. 2852.

[49] Medieval Chronicles, "Medieval Prince," accessed June 26, 2023, www.medievalchronicles.com/medieval-people/medieval-royalty/medieval-prince.

[50] Rev. R. O'Kennedy, *The Holy Angels* (Burnes & Oates Limited, 1887), 91.

[51] *Summa Theologica*, Art. 5, Obj. 6.

52 Horgan, *His Angels at Our Side*, 27.

53 Pseudo-Dionysius, *The Celestial and Ecclesiastical Hierarchy of Dionysius the Areopagite*, 9 as quoted in Parente.

54 Parente, *Angels in Catholic Teaching and Tradition*, 59.

55 *Catechism*, sec. 144.

56 Lk 1:34.

57 Lk 1:38.

58 Dictionary.com, accessed February 1, 2023, www.dictionary.com/browse/wrath.

59 Ps 37:8–9.

60 Eph 4:31–32.

61 Col 3:5–10.

62 Rom 1:18.

63 Rom 12:19.

64 Eph 4:26–27.

65 Prov 15:1–2.

66 Mt 26:51–54

67 Parente, *Angels in Catholic Teaching and Tradition*, 89.

68 Rev 1:11.

69 Tobit 12:11–15.

70 Parente, *Angels in Catholic Teaching and Tradition*, 111.

71 John 5:4.

72 Mike Auilina, *Angels of God: The Bible, the Church, and the Heavenly Hosts* (Servant Books, 2006), 69.

73 Mt 28:2–7.

74 1 Thess 4:16–17.

75 Parente, *Angels in Catholic Teaching and Tradition*, 90.

76 Rev 12:7–9.

77 *Diary*, 667.

78 Ibid., 630.

79 Ibid., 474–475.

80 Ibid., 471.

81 *Summa Theologica*, Art. 5, Obj. 4.

82 O'Connell, *Holy Angels*, 83.

83 *Angelic Spirituality: Medieval Perspectives on the Ways of Angels*, trans. Steven Chase (Paulist Press, 2002), 215–216.

84 Mt 13:40–43.

85 Mt 25:41.

86 *Butler's Lives of the Saints*, concise ed., ed. Michael Walsh (HarperSanFrancisco, 1991), 82–83.

87 *Catechism*, sec. 162.

[88] IrishCentral.com, "Saint Patrick's Breastplate: The Prayer of Ireland's Patron Saint," accessed May 3, 2023, www.irishcentral. com/roots/st-patricks-breastplate-prayer-irelands-patron-saint.

[89] *Catechism*, sec. 844.

[90] Ibid., sec. 2091.

[91] Ibid., sec. 1501.

[92] *Summa Theologica*, Art. 3, Obj. 2.

[93] Parente, *Angels in Catholic Teaching and Tradition*, 88.

[94] Ibid., 28–29.

[95] Mt 18:6–7.

[96] Mt 18:10–14.

[97] Ps 91:11–13.

[98] Horgan, *His Angels at Our Side*, 56.

[99] Mt 26:53.

[100] Horgan, *His Angels at Our Side*, 45.

[101] Ps 148:1–2.

[102] Lk 2:13–14.

[103] Horgan, *His Angels at Our Side*, 217.

[104] Ibid., 218–219.

[105] Ibid., 221–222.

[106] Ibid., 233–234.

[107] *Diary*, 314.

[108] Ibid., 828.

[109] Ibid., 412.

[110] Ibid., 419.

[111] *Catechism*, sec. 1821.

[112] Saint Teresa of Ávila, as quoted in *Catechism*, sec. 1821.

[113] *Catechism*, sec. 1772, 1764, 1765.

[114] John Henry Cardinal Newman, *Parochial and Plain Sermons*, vol. 2 (Longmans, Green, and Co., 1907), 21–22. See also *Catechism*, sec. 2142–2149.

[115] Mt 10:26–31.

[116] Mt 10:28.

[117] Peoplepill.com, "Antónia d'Astónaco," accessed February 8, 2023, peoplepill.com/people/antonia-dastonaco/.

[118] Saint Bernard of Clairvaux, *On Consideration*, Sermons on Psalm 90, V.5.12.

Essential Divine Mercy Resources

Diary of Saint Maria Faustina Kowalska:
Divine Mercy in My Soul

The *Diary* chronicles the message that Jesus, the Divine Mercy, gave to the world through this humble nun. In it, we are reminded to trust in His forgiveness — and as Christ is merciful, so, too, are we instructed to be merciful to others. Written in the 1930s, the *Diary* exemplifies God's love toward mankind and, to this day, remains a source of hope and renewal.

Large Paperback: Y119-NBFD
Compact Paperback: Y119-DNBF
Deluxe Leather-Bound Edition: Y119-DDBURG
Audio *Diary* MP3 Edition: Y119-ADMP3
 Also available as an ebook — Visit ShopMercy.org

Divine Mercy Catholic Bible

Many Catholics ask what version of the Bible is best to read. In the Revised Standard Version Catholic Edition (RSV-CE) you have the answer.

The *Divine Mercy Catholic Bible* clearly shows the astounding revelation of Divine Mercy amidst the timeless truths of Sacred Scripture. This Bible includes 175 Mercy Moments and 19 articles that explain how God encounters us with mercy through His Word and Sacraments. Leather-bound. 1,712 pages. Y119-BIDM

Explaining the Faith Series
Understanding Divine Mercy
by Fr. Chris Alar, MIC

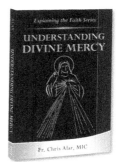

The entire Divine Mercy message and devotion is summarized in one, easy-to-read book! Explaining the teaching of Jesus Christ as given to St. Faustina, *Understanding Divine Mercy* by Fr. Chris Alar, MIC, has it all. Written in his highly conversational and energetic style, this first book in his *Explaining the Faith* series will deepen your love for God and help you understand why Jesus called Divine Mercy "mankind's last hope of salvation." Paperback. 184 pages.

Y119-EFBK

For our complete line of books, prayer cards, pamphlets, Rosaries, and chaplets, visit ShopMercy.org or call 1-800-462-7426 to have our latest catalog sent to you.

Pray for the Holy Souls in Purgatory

To Eternity
Y119-PFTD

Teaching Kids to
Pray for the Souls
in Purgatory
Y119-CLDPF

Heaven, Hell
& Purgatory
Y119-HHP

Explanation of
the St. Gertrude
Prayer
Y119-EOGPF
Prayer of
St. Gertrude
(prayer card)
Y119-SGPC11

An Introduction
to Indulgences
Y119-PIPF

The Four Daily
Plenary
Indulgences
Y119-DPIPF

Prayers with
Partial
Indulgences
Y119-INPF

Gregorian Masses
Y119-GMMPF

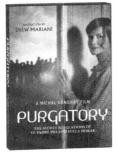

In this moving documentary, director Michal Kondrat ("Love and Mercy: Faustina") delves deeply into the evidence of science and mysticism (including the experiences of St. Padre Pio and St. Faustina) to offer a compelling summons to pray for the dead. Now with English voice-over. Y119-PDVD

CHAPLET OF ST. MICHAEL THE ARCHANGEL ROSARY

This set features a 15" chaplet of dark blue glass beads on silver-toned metal with a medallion of St. Michael with a Chaplet prayer and a laminated card of the Prayer to St. Michael. Y119-CHSM

Call 1-800-462-7426 or visit ShopMercy.org

Gems of Inspiration from Fr. Calloway!

Sacred Heart Gems
Daily Wisdom on the Heart of Jesus

There is no contradiction or competition between the message of the Sacred Heart as revealed to St. Margaret Mary Alacoque and the Divine Mercy message and devotion as revealed to St. Faustina. After all, it's the same Jesus! Father Calloway once again gathers a treasury of wisdom from blesseds, venerables, servants of God, and popes who loved the Sacred Heart. Each of the 366 days also contains an invocation from the Litany of the Sacred Heart of Jesus. Paperback. 304 pages. Y119-SHGM

Eucharistic Gems
Daily Wisdom on The Blessed Sacrament

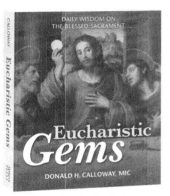

Eucharistic Gems is an aid to the Eucharistic Revival currently under way in the United States. What better way to make sure there always remains an on-going fruit of the Eucharistic Revival than to have a book that offers timeless quotes on the Eucharist — 366 quotes, in fact — from popes, saints, blessed, venerables, and servants of God? *Eucharistic Gems* is intended to be a book that can be read and re-read for years to come, and keep the Eucharistic Revival ever in our hearts. Paperback. 272 pages. Y119-EUGM

Rosary Gems
Daily Wisdom on the Holy Rosary
Y119-RGEM

Marian Gems
Daily Wisdom on Our Lady
Y119-MGEM

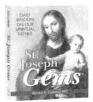

St. Joseph Gems
Daily Wisdom on our Spiritual Father
Y119-SJEM

Call 1-800-462-7426 or visit ShopMercy.org

Join the
Association of Marian Helpers,
headquartered at the
National Shrine of The Divine Mercy,
and share in special blessings!

**An invitation from
Fr. Joseph, MIC, the director**

**Marian Helpers is an Association of
Christian faithful of the Congregation
of Marian Fathers of the
Immaculate Conception.**
By becoming a member, you
share in the spiritual benefits
of the daily Masses, prayers,
and good works of the Marian
priests and brothers.

This is a special offer of grace
given to you by the Church
through the Marians. Please consider this opportunity to
share in these blessings, along with others whom you would
wish to join into this spiritual communion.

**The Marian Fathers of the Immaculate Conception of the
Blessed Virgin Mary is a religious congregation of nearly 500
priests and brothers around the world.**

Call 1-800-462-7426 or visit Marian.org